EXPLORING SOCIAL WORK

An Anthropological Perspective

Linda Bell

P

First published in Great Britain in 2020 by

Policy Press
University of Bristol
1-9 Old Park Hill
Bristol
BS2 8BB
UK
t: +44 (0)117 954 5940
pp-info@bristol.ac.uk
www.policypress.co.uk

North America office:
Policy Press
c/o The University of Chicago Press
1427 East 60th Street
Chicago, IL 60637, USA
t: +1 773 702 7700
f: +1 773-702-9756
sales@press.uchicago.edu
www.press.uchicago.edu

British Library Cataloguing in Publication Data
A catalogue record for this book is available from the British Library

Library of Congress Cataloging-in-Publication Data
A catalog record for this book has been requested

978-1-4473-5071-2 hardback
978-1-4473-5072-9 paperback
978-1-4473-5075-0 ePub
978-1-4473-5074-3 ePdf

Cover design by Robin Hawes
Front cover image: Andrey Popov, iStock

For Colin and Ray, who first introduced
me to the world of social work.

Contents

Acknowledgements

There are many people internationally whose support and wisdom over many years I have drawn upon when writing this book. This includes all the students from social work and other disciplines with whom I have worked, especially those who have attended social work qualifying programmes (particularly at Middlesex University, London) or who worked with me as doctoral students. My own PhD studies in anthropology were fundamental in enabling me to develop this book, so I must also thank those who were involved in my own education. I am grateful to all my academic colleagues and fellow researchers from various institutions, including all members of the international Qualitative Women's Workshop on Family/Household Research. Finally, I would like to thank all those I interviewed as key informants or research participants, as noted in the preface, without whom this book could not have been completed. I remain, of course, responsible for any mistakes or misinterpretations in the text.

I would particularly like to thank the following individuals from all the above areas: Lesley Adshead, Lucille Allain, Maria Ines Amâro, Diane Apeah-Kubi, Mary Baginsky, Jim Barry, Elisabeth Berg, Björn Blom, Nikki Bradley, Lene Ingemann Brandt, Karen Bryan, Kay Caldwell, Helena Carreiras, Edd Carter, Pat Cartney, Jessica Castillo, Luis Cavaco, John Chandler, Carmel Clancy, Christine Cocker, Andrew Cooper, Gina Copp, Helen Cosis-Brown, Nicolae-Adrian Dan, Yvonne Dhooge, Jean Dillon, Kingston Dire, Souzy Dracopoulou, Paul Dugmore, Jane Dutton, Ros Edwards, Marion Ellison, Leena Eskelinen, Lars Evertsson, Jorge Ferreira, Ann Flynn, Daniela Gaba, Tony Goodman, Trish Hafford-Letchfield, Nasreen Hammond, Sue Hanna, Elizabeth Harlow, Rosemary Harris, Teresa Harris, Hannah Henry Smith, Rachel Herring, Alison Higgs, Helen Hingley-Jones, Ray Holland, Mina Hyare, Jim Jenkins, Lesley Jordan, Ravi Kohli, Florin Lazăr, Lynne Lehane, Sarah Lewis-Brooke, Jane McCarthy, Lynn McDonald, Ken McLaughlin, Wilma Mangabeira, Oded Manor, Jane Maxim, Claudia Megele, Brian Melaugh, Sue Middleton, Rahaman Mohammed, Geoff Most, David Nilsson, Maria Appel Nissen, Chaim Noy, Linda Nutt, Sioban O'Farrell-Pearce, David Oliviere, Lesley Oppenheim, Rena Papadopoulos, Clare Parkinson, Jenny Pearce, Sian Peer, Marek Perlinski, Georgia Philip, Matthew Quaife, Karen Quinn, Katherine Rounce, Phil Slater, Theresa So, Adi Staempfli, Bismark Twumasi, Aase Villadsen, Jorunn Vindegg, Margaret Volante, Sandra Wallman, Rosslyn Webber, Gordon Weller,

Colin Whittington, Margaret Whittington, Tom Wilks, Barbara Winston, Maria Wolmesjö, Aidan Worsley.

Many thanks to Isobel, Sarah and all the team at Bristol University Press for your support, and thanks to the anonymous proposal and text referees.

Last but not least, thanks to my family – David, Tom and Sarah – for their patience and encouragement.

Preface

Many people have been instrumental in enabling me to write this book, including around 40 social workers and social work educators whom I formally interviewed over the past 12 years (either directly for this book in 2018, or as participants in various research projects). I have consciously included a range of workers, male and female, some of whom were working in front-line practice, some in management and some involved in social work education when they were interviewed; nearly all the social work educators had previously worked directly in practice. Some were very recently qualified, while others had been social workers for several years, with more than 30 years' experience in a few cases. Some informants were also keen researchers, and two were professors. Three were dual qualified (in nursing and social work). Some had additional specialist education/training, for example, in psychotherapy or legal work. A majority had trained as social workers and worked in England, but some had been trained abroad and subsequently worked in England ('transnationals'). Some of my informants had trained in Europe and continue to work there.

Whether quoting directly from this recent interview material or from other projects, I have taken steps to ensure that the person gave written consent to being interviewed according to current ethical good practice (see Miller and Bell, 2012). I and my research colleagues were granted formal research ethics approval from a university and/or local authorities as appropriate for specific projects that I discuss, including the recent set of informant interviews from 2018. I have anonymised any quotes as far as possible and allowed recent informants to see which quotes from their interviews I am using in the book wherever feasible.

My intention throughout this book has been to allow some UK and European-based social workers to express their views about the current prognosis for social work and the issues it currently has to address, as well as discussing their own experiences, looking back as far as the late 1980s/1990s. I also interweave my own experiences and thoughts about social work from the 1990s onwards. This is intended to help identify practices and underpinning values emerging from interviews and other research material. I call the chapters in this book mainly by active terms, such as 'Becoming', 'Identifying', 'Valuing' and so on, with the idea of building up a picture of social work incrementally in order to enable us to consider different viewpoints and experiences.

Introducing social work: who are social workers? Why do we need them?

'I think it is a positive future ... I think social workers have gained ground, although there's been a lot of, like, tragedies, blame and scandals ... they've actually also highlighted the role and the niche that social workers occupy, and made that more apparent, and the need ... social workers are needed when things like Grenfell[1] happen, or there's this big child abuse enquiry ... there is a level of skill and way of working that only social workers can provide ... as communities become more complex, as people's needs become more complex, so I think social work needs to keep changing along with society, and then it would always have a role.'

(Social worker, speaking in 2018)

I first came into contact with social work and social workers as an 'outsider' in the early 1990s; since then, I have worked extensively with social workers, social work educators and researchers. In this book, I will present and explore ideas about how, since that time, social workers have explained their practice in the UK and in other countries, especially in Europe, and how they, employers and the state organise and develop their professional education. I will suggest how I think these various activities influence the ways in which they see and act in the world.

I wanted to start this chapter by quoting some of the key informants who were prepared to give me their views about what they think 'social work' is, or claims to be, and why they think that society needs, or does not need, social workers. According to the opening account told to me as part of an interview with a social worker with many years of experience, who has also been involved with social workers' education, social change (including the difficulties encountered along the way) is particularly relevant to social work. The social and political contexts in which social work as an occupation is embedded are thus very likely to be key to any argument that stresses a need for social work and social workers. As we will see, 1989/1990 was a watershed for social work, especially across Europe, for all sorts of reasons, which was a key deciding factor in my choice of time period. I also discovered that Burnham's (2012) examination of social workers' own perspectives on their work and identities in the UK covered the period 1904 to 1989, so this reinforced my intention to focus on the time period since then.

Another underlying suggestion from this first informant's interview is that when, for various reasons, people find themselves in difficulties during their lives, social workers are not only those who feel compassion for these people, but also those who try to do something to assist. So, some kind of relationship between those who provide social work and those who are on the receiving end of social work support is also implied; furthermore, this is frequently a complicated issue. Social workers are trained, as this informant believes, with "*a level of skill and way of working that only social workers can provide*". In other words, social workers are not amateurs; they see themselves as professionals whose job (or, in some cases, they might say 'calling'[2]) compels them to act on their sense of compassion for others (or what some might nowadays term enabling 'social justice'; see, for example, Higgs, 2015). However, this is not to say that social work in all its forms is, or has always been, carried out by 'professionals' (a term that implies both specific forms of education and/or training, and also recognition of that professionalism by others). One key issue to be considered here is how the concept of 'profession' itself is viewed (see, for example, Dent and Whitehead, 2002); earlier commentators have questioned whether social work should be seen as a full profession.[3]

All these points suggest some degree of disjunction between the people that we may think of as social workers and social work itself, with both terms being multi-layered. Speaking as an anthropologist (of which more later), I have tried to explore first of all (from the outside) how this short extract from an interview with a social worker can start to build up a picture, with many implications, for us to try and understand social work and what it means to be a social worker.

The first account implies that there will always be a need for society/ies to employ (or to permit) people to take up a role in social work, or as what we may term a 'social worker'. A second account from another social worker also refers to some of the political and structural barriers to social workers being able to act on their sense of what they would term 'social justice'. In reviewing these first two full interviews, I could see that both informants shared a strong commitment to social work, even though their stated prognosis for the occupation may seem superficially different. This second social worker, also speaking in 2018 about social work in the UK, thought that:

> '*the role of social work has diminished over the years and that's for a variety of different reasons, and I think they're partly to do with neoliberalism and the expectation that the population are independent and dependency is discouraged. So, any long-term arrangements which might have existed in the past between vulnerable individuals, or families, or communities and social work are actively discouraged. And I also think that connects with the reduction of the welfare state and the reduced amount of money that's available for services, and I think social workers have generally worked with the more vulnerable communities, the communities or the individuals that are marginal in various ways, whereas the investment now is on the universal services, education and health. I think we've become an investment state, so the idea is that the state, rather than providing welfare, will invest in individuals and families so that they become independent and live independently, and don't make any demands. So, I think, partly, social work has shifted its status as a result of that.*'

In examining this second extract, we can begin to see exactly how another (equally) experienced informant embeds social work within relevant social policy and political contexts. This interview extract suggests that the prevailing political climate in recent years (in particular, the spread of neoliberalism) has altered the relationship of the state to social work and to citizens in general (a view shared by many; see, for example, Hughes and Lewis, 1998; Ferguson, 2008; Spolander et al, 2014). The informant suggests that this has taken place via reductions in the acceptability of social welfare and a greater emphasis being placed on both individual freedom and individual responsibility. This also implies that there is a tension between notions of universal services and those that may be targeted at those in society who are seen as marginal or vulnerable in some way.

In order to underline the point about the changing political and policy terrains within which social workers in England and elsewhere have to work (which I will address in more detail in the following chapters), an extract from a third informant's interview spells out some of the differences between how this informant thinks social work *was* when she entered the profession in the early 1990s and how she sees the state of social work *now*. This third informant's stated ideas also connect to more specific locational and organisational aspects of doing social work *then* and *now*:

> '*there's been a huge shift in terms of prevention*[4] *and also in terms of geography. Back then* [in the 1990s], *social work services were located in the communities they were serving, so they were ... I started off across the road from my council estate, it was open, people would come in and out. I mean people didn't necessarily welcome social workers, but it was a point of contact, and many local authorities now have taken services out of the community and put them in really quite inaccessible places, where if you're an older person, or an adult with a disability, or a parent with kids in a buggy, you're never, ever physically going to get there. So, we've been removed from the people that we serve and I think that's wrong. I think we should be part of the community, we should be co-located in health clinics, in hospitals, in libraries. It should be a much more open environment.*'

This same informant also identified differences between different parts of the UK with which she has experience:

> '*I think there are huge problems also with the ageing population and the health and social care interface, and especially in England. It's not the same in Scotland; there's far more services for older people to stay at home. In England, the services are being cut to the bone and families are being left to struggle and there is no proper provision for social care.*'

Although social work and social workers can thus be described in various ways (especially by those involved, as we shall see throughout this book), the preceding quotes initially suggest that practice or action involving people with various social problems is usually seen as a central issue for social work, not least by social workers themselves (see also the July 2014 definition of the International Federation of Social Workers [IFSW][5]). These people may be defined (by social workers and by the rest of society) as 'marginal' or 'vulnerable' in some way, although the global definition also stresses 'principles of social justice, human rights, collective responsibility and respect for diversities', which also implies universal needs and rights at some levels.[6]

A fourth ('transnational'[7]) informant, who has worked in the UK and elsewhere in Europe, explicitly linked these issues to wider political regimes and to the overall existence of social work when he suggested: "*I think social work is really a function of a capitalist state because of the kind of way it's organised* [for]… *the victims of that economic system*" (Social worker, speaking in 2018). This introduces a further, basic notion, widespread throughout social work literature and in practice, that in many ways social work is about both caring and controlling.

Social work: addressing the taken for granted

Taking up an outsider perspective, as I aim to do in this book, we should note that Harris (2008: 662–3) also suggests that we should be wary of any prevailing taken-for-granted assumptions about (state) social work and social workers:

> If we had never encountered state social work as an institution and never been prepared for the role it plays in our culture, on first acquaintance we might find the idea of designated strangers meeting and talking with people about intimate aspects of those people's lives quite odd. However, this practice and the institutions that support it are not usually seen as anything out of the ordinary; social work occupies a cultural position in which the most common response to questions about its nature and purpose is simply to see it as a straightforward response to self-evident human needs and problems.

Everyone seems to have something to say about social work and social workers, and this occupational group is often highlighted in the popular press and scrutinised negatively in relation to political issues and social policies, both in the UK and internationally. This kind of response also has the potential to reinforce negative discourses about welfare and recipients of welfare. Some observers seem to go out of their way to demonise those who work in the social work and social care fields; this not only produces one-sided accounts, but may also result in a defensive response from social workers and social work educators. For example, Edmondson and King's (2016: 639) analysis of social workers appearing in UK television and film dramas suggests that their work is mainly focused on child protection and child removal, and that they are often portrayed in these dramas as 'incompetent, bureaucratic, well-meaning but misguided'.

Yet, currently, within UK higher education and in UK workplaces, education and training to become a social worker can hardly have been more popular, a trend receiving tacit state support via recent educational changes aimed at increasing their numbers. Reviewing social workers' current professional preoccupations internationally through many and varied publications, reports and documents, as I have tried do while writing this book, reveals concepts and statements of values such as 'compassion' and 'social justice', as well as a focus on the social and sometimes psychosocial: working through relationships, reflexivity/reflectivity and use of self. However, as Harris (2008: 663) points out, social work is sometimes seen as simply 'a component in a process of steady and inevitable progress towards a more humane society ... [in which] social work is envisaged as a humanitarian reflex action'. For those who would accept this view, does 'steady and inevitable progress' also imply that (formally constituted) social work is only relevant to certain kinds of societies, or to certain classes or groups of people? As I began my own journey with social workers in the early 1990s, social policy academics and others were already writing about a crisis in care and challenges to social work, which was seen as having inherent ambiguities in terms of its aims to both care and control, with regards to what social work *is* and what it *does*, and with all the social pressures that this implies (see Clarke, 1993).

Apart from social workers themselves, in Western societies where social work has become established, those who may want or need social work interventions or, as some people prefer, services[8] should surely be included among those who can help to control its practice, education and training. There are certainly differing views about the kind of influence that users of social work services ought to have in the creation of new social workers. Since 1990, in tandem with contemporary policy changes around, for example, Community Care (and related splits into 'purchasing' and 'providing' of both services and education/training; see Chapters 3, 4 and 10, this volume), 'service user' influences have generally become more accepted and expected[9] (for changing perspectives over time, see, for example, Hugman, 1991; Beresford, 1994; CCETSW, 1997; Beresford et al, 2008; Matka et al, 2010; Tanner et al, 2017). We should also notice (inter)subjectivities here, as expressed by various users of services, where personal characteristics or interests may overlap.[10] This also brings us to the whole issue of social work being perceived as a female and 'caring profession', or perhaps 'semi-profession' (see, for example, McPhail, 2004; see also discussions of feminist approaches in especially Chapters 2, 5 and 6, this volume).

As I explain further in Chapter 2, a key reason for writing this book through an anthropological lens is that although I have had over 25 years of association with social work and, in particular, social work education,

I still consider myself to be an outsider. Initially, this outsider identity as an anthropologist was, I know, seen as advantageous to the social work project that I first became involved with in 1991 (particularly in terms of reflexivity and elements relating to inter-professional working). However, as time went by, I began to understand how I and others could construct different understandings around social work, grounded in various epistemological and theoretical perspectives, and tease out the increasing complexity of those perspectives; meanwhile, my own subsequent outsider positioning and identification has not always been easy or comfortable to maintain, as we will see later.

There are evidently many important policy-based influences on social work coming from outside, not least from the state in various settings, as well as from other professions/occupations. These contexts, including selected international examples, will also be explored in this book, especially in Chapters 3 and 10; however, a wider overall focus on international social work, with its strong emphasis on globalisation *per se*, cannot be my main concern here, and this topic has also been written about extensively elsewhere (see, for example, Gray and Fook, 2004; Healey and Link, 2011).

In using all my material, I will argue that social work, seen as occupation *and* as identity (or set of identities), reveals specific cultural and symbolic representations that can widen our insights into the impacts that these professionals have on society/ies, and how states and social contexts can shape the profession, both positively and negatively. This book tries to go beyond simply *describing* social workers as a 'professional group', whether nationally or internationally.

In Chapter 2, I will discuss how and why I am taking up a specifically anthropological perspective in this book. Chapter summaries will be given at the end of each of the chapters.

Chapter 1 summary

This chapter introduces social work and social workers and has begun to explore the following questions: what is social work and who are social workers? How do we address the taken-for-granted nature of social work? What influences do the state, social policy and public perceptions (including users of social work services) have on social work? I include some extracts taken from recent interviews with workers about social work as they have experienced it in the past and the present, and how they view its future prognosis. This introductory chapter also outlines the outsider approach that I am taking to exploring social work.

Notes

[1] The Grenfell Tower fire in London 2017.

[2] For a psychological 'take' on this concept, see, for example, Hall and Chandler (2005).

[3] 'Scholars writing at the end of the 1960s labelled it a semi-profession because it either lacked certain traits considered essential to a fully-fledged profession (e.g. professional autonomy) or these traits had not yet fully developed.... Since the 1980s, as its knowledge base had developed, social work has been described as an "emerging" or "developing" profession' (Weiss-Gal and Welbourne, 2008: 282).

[4] In other words, moving from a focus on preventive social work to a more specific focus on targeted, or crisis, forms of intervention.

[5] 'Social work is a practice-based profession and an academic discipline that promotes social change and development, social cohesion, and the empowerment and liberation of people. Principles of social justice, human rights, collective responsibility and respect for diversities are central to social work. Underpinned by theories of social work, social sciences, humanities and indigenous knowledge, social work engages people and structures to address life challenges and enhance wellbeing. The above definition may be amplified at national and/or regional levels' (International Federation of Social Workers (IFSW), 2014).

[6] We should also note that responses to the IFSW definition show that it is contested by some social workers (see, for example, Ornellas et al, 2018).

[7] I take this definition from Hussein (2014).

[8] To an anthropologist, the language used in this context often speaks volumes about how these activities are regarded: 'interventions' speak of something being 'done to' someone, but also of research and (some would argue) credibility. 'Services' may sound old-fashioned and might also be seen as a sort of 'gift' to the recipient. A particular dislike of mine is the more recent and businesslike (Managerialist?) term 'offer', as in 'our offer to clients' (of rehabilitation, of different kinds of care packages and so on), all dependent on the availability of resources.

[9] However, researchers have reported varied outcomes from such involvement, and some (for example, Webber and Robinson, 2012) have suggested that such involvement is also less visible at the post-qualifying level of social work education.

[10] A relevant connection here to change within the history of feminist thought has been the moves from earlier 'feminist standpoint' perspectives (represented by thinkers such as Sandra Harding, Nancy Hartsock or Alison Jaggar), epistemologies arguably dominated by white, middle-class feminists, towards a more inclusive focus on various intersubjectivities, embracing different ethnicities, (dis)abilities, sexualities and so on.

2

Getting involved: an anthropological and auto-ethnographic journey

To the complex mixture of ideas and questions about social work coming from social workers and others that I identified in Chapter 1, I wanted to add some of my own experiences and reflections as anthropological and auto-ethnographic elements throughout the book; these will include material from specific research projects that I have conducted myself or with colleagues. I hope that these more personal aspects will inject some sense of trajectory (As well as indicating frustration and, on occasions, humour!) as I have gradually worked towards trying to understand social work and social workers. I hope that, in doing so, this may engage others who have tried to do the same. These initial ideas set me thinking about my own journey into the world of social work, which goes back more than 25 years. In the following, I describe what first happened to me in the early 1990s.

Encountering social work: a surprising discovery[1]

One day in July 1991, I walked up the hill from the high street in a London neighbourhood to attend a job interview. I had seen a newspaper advertisement for a research post and, being a part-time PhD student in anthropology with two young children, I decided to apply, mainly in order to broaden my research experience and earn some money. The post concerned research into social work, organisations and what was termed 'inter-professional working'.

At that time, I knew next to nothing about social work, although my anthropological research concerned families in England with young children. This might seem surprising but my (fairly narrow) PhD research focus was on family networks and social support between mothers, and the (mainly middle-class) families that I had been working with were largely involved in voluntary groups such as playgroups and nurseries run by organisations such as the Pre-School Playgroups Association (PPA). These organisations mainly had contacts with health staff, particularly health visitors and general practitioners (GPs) (what, with hindsight, we might term 'universal services'). Nobody had ever mentioned social work or social workers to me during the earlier part of my research, which, I now realise, must have been either an omission (Because I was not looking?) or more likely the potentially stigmatising 'elephant in the room' that no one else wanted to talk about (this was also the reaction of a social work academic whom I interviewed much more recently).

My friends and colleagues, who were also researching within the fields of anthropology and sociology at that time, did not talk much about social work either. We were all academics with academic interests and, at that time, a few of these people were actively hostile to the idea that research should be applied to something like social work, which seemed to suggest an ethos of 'telling people how to run their lives'. On the other hand, I had previously been a member of a group (at one stage) called British Association for Anthropology in Policy and Practice (BASAPP),[2] which promoted the idea that anthropology should be useful, not only in far-flung places, but also here 'at home'. I was, in short, an idealist.

All this meant that I walked into my first direct encounter with social work (or, at least, social work research) with interest but also holding a few preconceptions. I felt that I wanted my own research to be useful to society somehow and I thought that it should not only be about academic excellence; nevertheless, I was unsure whether 'social work' would be relevant to me.

The three people on the interview panel (a woman and two men) were engaging and talked with enthusiasm about their project[3]; later, I found out that the woman interviewer had been asked to join the panel to cover certain aspects of the post and that she was not directly part of the research team. I also assumed that they were all social workers but it turned out that one of the men was an academic who worked closely with social workers as a researcher. The more they talked, the more I found this to be fascinating stuff, and I was soon 'hooked'. Later that evening, I was telephoned and offered the post. I probably did not realise until much later that it is very much in the social work ethos to build up the confidence of those with whom you are working, and once I started in the job and got to know everyone, it seemed that I had not necessarily been the preferred candidate. So, my arrival into social work territory was surprising all round.

Encountering social work by an indirect route

It was perhaps fortunate that when I first encountered social work, it was obliquely backlit for me as an occupation by being identified specifically in relation to other professionals: the study that I was to join had a focus, in part, on social workers' preparation for inter-professional working (for more details, see Whittington, 1998; Whittington and Bell, 2001). This was also a theme that dominated my own thinking for several years and it remained part of my intellectual remit while I subsequently began my university teaching career with students of social work and other health- and social-care occupations.

The related context that emerged from that initial research project was organisational; in other words, social work might, and I believe does, inevitably differ depending on *where* and *how* social workers are employed.[4] Whittington (1998), whose project I had joined in 1991, has written in detail (in his doctoral thesis and other publications) about the relevance of organisational and inter-professional contexts, as well as of the possibilities for, and issues with, the development of a 'professional project' in social work.

Box 2.1: Why a focus on contexts?

An interesting point emerged in 1992 while we were receiving survey responses to the 'CCETSW-King's College' (C-K) project: in a note on their completed questionnaire, one respondent asked us why there was a need to consider these inter-professional and organisational contexts at all when the most important thing (for this respondent at any rate) was the relationship between the social worker and client. That, the respondent thought, should have been the focus of our study!

My colleagues reassured me that, of course, a key reason that our project had been framed in the way in which it had been was because few people had previously focused directly on these contextual aspects, and for me, these contexts did, indeed, help to identify social work as a live, communicating entity that had (I decided) much to contribute to society. By focusing on the contextual framework, social work (however defined) could then come out of those shadows more clearly.

With hindsight, and from revisiting the pages of *The British Journal of Social Work* for 1991 and 1992, it is clear that inter-professional and, to some extent, organisational issues and contexts were starting to be researched, and that this was particularly relevant in view of the policy changes around that time in all aspects of social work (see especially the Children Act 1989 and the NHS and Community Care Act, 1990; see also Chapters 3 and 4, this volume).

Why take an *anthropological* perspective on social work?

At this point, I should expand a little more about my anthropological perspective(s) when writing this book. Anthropologists have usually tried to work with people from what they would see as an 'outsider' perspective, exploring aspects of what we might initially regard as the taken-for-granted aspects of culture. However, I am aware that there is a danger, especially given the colonial origins of some forms of anthropology, that some anthropologists may have been working with a sense of their own power when trying to explain the 'strange' practices of 'their people', especially when seeking (cross-)cultural representation.

In his book examining history and theory in anthropology, Alan Barnard (2000: 177) writes that anthropology itself might more usefully and meaningfully be seen as 'a discourse on the human condition, played out in a dialogue between those under the scrutiny of anthropologists on the one hand, and anthropologists themselves on the other'. In accepting this statement, I am trying to find out from people identifying as social workers: 'what they say' (in this case, about their work, their sense of identity and so on); 'what they do' (for example, in everyday practice or education); and 'what they say they do' (explaining to outsiders *why* they do what they do, their values and so on). This approach may seem somewhat formulaic, but in my defence, I hope to at least avoid jumping to unwarranted conclusions. I realise the need to make some interpretations of my own about social work cultural representations, broadly covering areas such as *language*, *actions* or *symbols*, but I also want to check with various informants what their perspectives are. This way of working 'in dialogue' with people thus becomes a delicate balancing act, and includes exploring the impact that social work has had on me over the years, as well as taking account of the (perhaps more familiar) implications for users/ receivers of social work services, or, indeed, for other professionals who work with social workers. As Pálsson (1993: 37) suggests, I am aiming to follow an approach that we might characterise as a 'living discourse' in which 'anthropologists immerse themselves in a democratic ethnographic dialogue with the people they visit, forming an intimate rapport or communion and representing the experience as a moment in the stream of life'.

Furthermore, while I am scrutinising (or 'othering'?) social workers, they are surely doing the same to their service users/clients, to me and to their work colleagues (see also Chapter 8, this volume). We might therefore see Barnard's and Pálsson's characterisations of anthropological discourse as not simply being two-way, but also going in multiple, exploratory directions.

Some people have already written anthropological accounts while *working within social work* or *welfare*, using ethnographic or auto-ethnographic techniques in the main and identifying practice with different groups of people (see, for example, Edgar and Russell, 2005; Witkin, 2014). Other anthropologists have been concerned with, for example, *seeking solutions* to the need for care (Alber and Drotbohm, 2015) in order to directly address *contemporary human problems*; this may include wider aspects of economics, poverty, power, politics, the environment, social conflict and so on, as well as focusing on key issues of cultural diversity (see, for example, Bodley, 2012). The direct anthropological search for solutions to problems is largely outside the scope of this book. However, I have participated in a few projects addressing social work-focused action and intervention that I will discuss at various points in this book. I agree with Harris (2008) that there is a need to address the perhaps taken-for-granted aspects of the practices and philosophy/ies lying behind social work when exploring how people become, practise and identify as social workers.

What social worker colleagues might thus identify, as part of the dialogue between us, as my reflexive (or reflective) positioning (see Holland, 1999; Cartney, 2015) as an anthropologist, coming from *outside social work*, is therefore fundamental to this book. I consider my approach as in keeping with recent approaches to social anthropology,[5] and in researching my material, I have drawn not only upon published literature, but also on my own research, which has used established anthropological and sociological, qualitative and quantitative methods, including the use of documentary analysis, interviews (see Hockey, 2002, 2014), (participant) observation and ethnography, as well as some auto-ethnographic[6] techniques (Ellis and Bochner, 2000; Ellis et al, 2011). There is some useful epistemological overlap in what lies beneath some of these methods, as the anthropologist Jenny Hockey (2014: 93) has written: 'when western, anthropologists-at-home do opt for single time bounded interviews, their practice may in fact resemble many of the social interactions that constitute everyday life for their participants. As such they can be considered precisely a form of participant observation'.

In terms of my own anthropological background, I first studied anthropology in the UK in the 1970s via a wide-ranging (BSc) degree course at University College London that combined social and physical/biological anthropology, archaeology, and material culture. This was what first gave me an interest in exploring various epistemological positions, interpretivist as well as more positivistic, structuralist or functionalist approaches. I had also trained and worked as a professional librarian. However, such an eclectic background made it hard at first to discern my own theoretical direction as an anthropologist, apart from having an overall interest in what I then thought of as 'culture(s)'.[7]

Further anthropological study at doctoral level (Bell, 1995) and working as a research assistant with colleagues on projects relating to urban anthropology in London during the 1980s (see Wallman, 1984) did enable me to more clearly establish the kinds of theoretical issues and positions that I wished to pursue. I had become wary of processes of 'othering' that seemed to be attached to many of the earlier, more colonial, forms of anthropological enquiry, and that seemed to suggest an unhelpful hierarchy of societies and social forms. This realisation, in turn, reinforced my ideas about the possibility of using anthropological ideas and methods within all kinds of societies and social groupings, and thus being able to examine relevant issues such as power, including the power of professional workers in society (for the relevance of exploring *capacity*, *context* and *communication* to this kind of anthropological enquiry, see also Wallman, 1997).

My own PhD research work with mothers and families, and subsequent involvement with feminist research and writing (including long-standing membership of a women's research group[8]), gave me an enduring interest in critical and emancipatory forms of enquiry, so that once I encountered social work (which some have considered as a female-dominated occupation[9]), I felt that I already had a potential connection with those who identify as social workers. At the same time I became fascinated by the ways in which these professionals themselves seemed to be wielding some kinds of power within society/ ies (and, conversely, how society/ies seemed to be controlling or manipulating them, wherever they worked). I have felt, for example, that there seems to be a tension between the crucial relationships that social workers (with the 'power'?) have with those with whom they tend to work ('vulnerable', 'marginalised'?) and other people in society, including their colleagues (for an earlier exploration of the emancipatory potential of professional social work, see also Hugman, 1991).

Taking these issues further, I have also found the term(s) 'identity/ ies' and 'identification' useful as sociological concepts, particularly in relation to professional and work contexts (see, for example, Jenkins, 2014; Chandler, 2017). Jenkins and Chandler usefully draw our attention to both *individual* and *collective* forms of identity (for further discussion of identity, see also Chapter 6, this volume). This has implications for social workers, as Spolander and colleagues (2014: 309) have suggested: 'The role of individual practitioners and citizens should not be underestimated, but social work needs to be more visible, critical, promote debate as well as critical pedagogy'.

Turning to the term 'culture', while still useful in some respects, this is sometimes quite vague when further examined, as the anthropologist Adam Kuper (2000) has pointed out; and, when used in a deterministic way and associated with power, this can lead to oppressive practices, for example, if individuals become forced into *identifying with* 'their' culture in specific ways. So, searching for some sort of overarching and unified social work culture seems to do little except put tenuous and ambiguous boundaries around this occupation/profession (again, see the definition of the International Federation of Social Workers [IFSW]). On the other hand, Bourdieu's notion of 'habitus' can prove useful[10] in relation to social work and social workers in terms of a focus on identities (as mentioned earlier) since, as Barnard (2000: 142) suggests, this 'theory of practice' lies 'between the objective and the subjective, the collective and the individual. It is culturally defined, but its locus is the mind of the individual. Habitus is a kind of structure of social action by culturally competent performers'.

Underpinning themes: approaches to social work

During my first involvement in the collaborative C-K project from 1991 onwards, I quickly became aware of the theoretical and disciplinary underpinnings of social work connecting to a diverse range of social sciences, including law, sociology and psychology, as well as anthropology (as also indicated in the current IFSW definition). My project colleagues, writing from sociological and psychosocial perspectives, initially provided me with a framework of theoretical approaches to social work that they had devised and published, derived from the work of the sociologists Burrell and Morgan (Burrell and Morgan, 1979; Whittington and Holland, 1985; Holland, 1999). This was helpful in first suggesting to me (in terms of a meta-theoretical or 'bird's-eye view' approach) that not all social workers thought, still less practised, in the same way(s). Holland (1999) has connected this approach to *reflexivity* in more depth to Kuhn (2012) and also to the anthropologist Mary Douglas, with whose work I was already familiar (for example, Douglas, 1999, 1986; see also Chapter 11, this volume).

These paradigmatic themes, especially when mapped in diagrammatic form as a matrix (see Whittington and Holland, 1985;

Holland, 1999), reveal, for example, the underlying philosophical roots of some social workers who may define themselves as 'radicals' (including some who may take up feminist approaches), while there are others who have perhaps trained and actively work within particular theoretical positions, such as taking a psychoanalytic/psychodynamic approach. Although some social researchers have posited a general divide reflecting functionalist versus interpretivist approaches (not to mention qualitative and quantitative research methods) (see also Bell, 2017) , as well as tensions between evidence-based and relationship-based approaches to professional practice and to research, I would argue that the situation is much more complex than simple binary divisions (see Holland, 1999). Instead, we need to explore all of these possible aspects, especially for an understanding of social work research (for further discussions of some of these differing approaches, see Chapter 9, this volume).

At this point, I should indicate that following my initial social work research post, I went on to work as a lecturer, mainly teaching research methods to social work students but also working with nurses and other professional students. I have also been engaged in consultancy work for an educational regulator and have been involved in various health- and social care-related research projects. Having already been introduced to differing approaches to social work research and practice I then began to witness, during my academic career, ambiguities and some defensiveness coming from those social workers trying to promote a particular stance (sometimes for my benefit), or what they might see as a more unified social work way of thinking, valuing or doing things. An early response of mine to such ambiguities had been to construct a conference paper with my own metaphorical and deliberately ambiguous vision of social work education and training, simultaneously representing a (defensive) 'castle' and a (collaborative) 'bridge' (Bell, 1994, 2007b). While I acknowledge that I may have been somewhat confused at that stage, I needed to try and spell out, using this metaphor, why this was!

Acknowledging all these ambiguities was one reason why, in my recent book on research methods for social workers (Bell, 2017), I suggested that when doing research, social workers could broaden their outlook(s) to 'Look beyond narrow definitions of "social work" or "social work research" to include wider multi-disciplinary approaches, including those from disciplines such as psychology, social policy or sociology; this is particularly useful where these connect with social workers' practice concerns and values embracing social justice, partnership or participatory approaches' (Bell, 2017: 172–3).

I also think that we need to remain aware of the differing settings and countries within which social work takes place, as well as of the various schools of thought that underpin social work activities and the differing ways in which social workers are educated/socialised in different places. I have explored these issues myself through involvement in some international conferences and co-writing, and have gained further insights through talking with, and also formally interviewing, some social workers not based in the UK and a few who have come to work in the UK from elsewhere. I thus intended to draw upon a diverse range of approaches to research material for this book.

An eclectic stance has also proved useful when exploring social workers' processes of socialisation and their developing attitudes to research and what has been termed 'evidence-based' practice (see especially Chapters 4, 5 and 9, this volume). As a comparative, professional example covering (social) relationships and clinical evidence, the anthropologist Good's (1994) text demonstrates how medical education and practice can 'construct' doctors and their views of the body. Good (1994: 68) suggests that we can view medicine as a *symbolic form* 'through which reality is formulated and organized in a distinctive manner' (see also Chapter 11, this volume). He goes on to say that in medicine, 'Healing activities shape the objects of therapy ... and seek to transform those objects through therapeutic activities' (Good, 1994: 68) (for a discussion of *symbolism* in relation to social work, see Chapter 11, this volume).

Coming back to the beginning of Chapter 1, what of social workers' own voices in all of this? Jean Gordon's very recent paper (2018: 1345–6) suggests that the 'significance of the social worker's voice to policy making, practice and, crucially, to outcomes for service users and carers is only just starting to be understood'. This does surprise me a little. Clearly, there have been numerous research studies about social workers' practice and their explanations of that practice, yet Gordon asserts that the social worker's 'voice' is absent or at least under-represented in terms of (its) impact. However, does this argument assume that there is a unified voice? Moreover, how is that voice to be constituted? As one of my recent interviewees put it when I asked about current issues for social work:

> '*the profession as a whole does not speak with one voice ... so it's the lack of a large, or majority, organisation to speak for social work, if you compare that with the United States, with the National Association for Social Work, or in Australia or New Zealand,*

where they are absolutely clear that social work is a profession.'
(Social worker, speaking in England, 2018)

This informant also introduces the idea of organisation as being somehow linked to voice and therefore to representation (for an official view of this issue from 2009, see also Department for Children, Schools and Families, 2009).[11] However this issue of voice is framed, a focus on the use of *language* by social workers is valuable here (whether directly as speech or in terms of written materials). The apparent absence of social workers' voice is one reason why I decided, among other appropriate methods, to make use of what anthropologists have called 'key informants', whose words will help to inform and guide this overall narrative, as in the example just given. I would say that we need to *hear* those voices (and also discern the (multiple) identities) of social workers as they go about their business(es), and to *listen* to them as they explain their work and their perspectives (see also Cree and Davis, 2007). However, I should also recognise that, in doing this, I am trying to identify not one voice, but multiple voices and views.

Exploration of social work in terms of its history, legislation and related social policy developments since about 1990, which I address next in Chapter 3, soon reveals how social work is significantly embedded within different kinds of social and policy contexts. There has been continuing discussion about social workers as agents of the state in this regard (as noted in some of the earlier interview quotes), but many social workers themselves seem to imply that 'real social work' (whether in its caring or controlling elements) is mainly about their relationships with those whom they serve. I had very little experience in the early 1990s of how social workers actually worked, and what their thoughts were about 'why they did what they did'. Politically, some tensions and signs of difficulty were already there, before and after 1990 (a date that, with hindsight, appears as a watershed on many levels, in the UK as well as elsewhere). I noted then that suggestions for future developments in the early 1990s included how to address power issues between social workers and those with whom they work (see particularly Hugman, 1991).

Chapter 2 summary

I explain my own positioning and how anthropologists try to work from an outsider perspective. I include some ideas about different theoretical perspectives about social work. My reflexive positioning as an anthropologist is fundamental to this book and I argue that my approach is in keeping with recent methodological and theoretical approaches to social anthropology. This chapter begins to provide some auto-ethnographic background relating to my longitudinal work with social workers and social work educators in the UK; this will also allow me to critically reflect on my own position. Finally in this chapter, I address the issue of social work 'voice' and representation.

Notes

[1] It should be noted that, for clarity, I place direct quotes from informants in italics.

[2] See, for example, the paper by Shore and Wright (1996: 475), who point out, perhaps rather unnecessarily, that 'In general ... anthropologists do not enjoy a high public profile in the life of the nation'.

[3] This became known as the 'CCETSW-King's College' (C-K) project. It included a survey of the final cohorts of the 1990 Certificate in Social Service (CSS) and Certificate of Qualification in Social Work (CQSW) programmes in the Central Council for Education and Training in Social Work's (CCETSW's) London and South-East England region (see Whittington, 1998; Whittington and Bell, 2001).

[4] Harris (2008: 663) describes social work as 'a contingent activity' (see also Chapter 3, this volume).

[5] See also Chapter 11 on 'Symbolising', including a discussion of recent approaches in anthropology such as materialist analyses (Miller, 2009) and the ontological turn (see Todd, 2016; Holbraad and Pedersen, 2017; Cepek, 2019).

[6] 'Autoethnography is an approach to research and writing that seeks to describe and systematically analyze personal experience in order to understand cultural experience.... Thus, as a method, autoethnography is both process and product' (Ellis et al, 2011: 273).

[7] For useful historical and epistemological narratives of various branches of anthropology see Barnard (2000) and Kuper (2000, 2016).

[8] The Women's Workshop (see Ribbens and Edwards (eds), 1998; Gillies and Lucey (eds), 2007; Mauthner et al, (eds) 2012; Weller and Rogers (eds), 2012; Philip and Bell, 2017).

[9] However, see McPhail (2004), who suggests that if an occupation consists mainly of female rank-and-file members but they 'lack power and control', this does not make it 'female-dominated'.

[10] See also the edited volume by Adkins and Skeggs (2004), which takes aspects of Bourdieu's work, including attention to the notion of reflexivity, in feminist directions.

[11] The Social Work Task Force explicitly suggested that social workers should develop a more powerful voice that would allow them to raise their status and their credibility when working with other relevant partners (see Department for Children, Schools and Families, 2009: 11).

Time and change: UK social work and comparative European welfare policies since 1990

> *'the one constant thing in social work is that it's always changing.'*
> (Social worker, speaking in 2018)

> It is important that social work keeps a sense of being on the cusp, aware of the constraints and contradictions, moving forwards but never expecting to arrive. That is the key to an understanding that is both optimistic and realistic.
> (Dickens, 2011: 36)

Introduction

In the previous chapters, we identified that social and political change provides an essential foundation for how social work has developed, and how social workers are able (or perhaps unable) to act, in different places. This was indicated by the views and experiences of the key informant social workers and social work educators whom I have quoted in Chapters 1 and 2. Taking an anthropological perspective towards social work itself surely requires exploring contexts and chronology, especially in terms of changing professional and policy discourses.

Following up on these themes as expressed in published research and other documentary sources in this chapter (see, for example, University of Warwick, 2012; Burnham, 2011; Burnham, 2012), Harris (2008: 663, emphasis added), for example, sets out to counter:

> [the] commonly encountered view of social work as a straightforward and widening response to human needs over time. Rather, in the account ... provided, social work is regarded as having developed in particular conditions and in response to particular pressures; in other words, social work is a *contingent activity*, conditioned by and dependent upon the *context* from which it emerges and in which it engages.

For an anthropologist, the suggestion that social work inevitably has a contingent nature is an interesting and, I believe, useful starting point when examining policy and legislative issues and changes. My own gradual introduction to 'social work' in different places and times after 1990 also leads me to think that whether following up on social work education, 'socialisation', actions and 'interventions', or even social work 'values', I have not always and everywhere been walking along exactly 'the same' paths. Furthermore, while sometimes exciting, these experiences could also lead me personally into misunderstandings, wrong-footedness and insecurities. I think that social workers themselves (and those who come into contact with them) must also experience similar uncertainties, unless these changes can perhaps be anticipated and accommodated, 'being aware of the constraints and contradictions' can thus be seen as a strength rather than a weakness, as Dickens (2011) suggested earlier. Sheppard (1998) also usefully drew attention to the dangers of unrestrained 'relativism' in social work contexts, where theoretical or practical alternatives are being considered.

In this chapter, I will give a brief outline narrative to some key political and economic developments affecting 'social work', beginning with a general overview of welfare regimes across Europe. I will next briefly describe these changes in the UK during the 20th century, involving many policy-related, legislative, economic and political developments still implicit today, including an increasing focus on risk (see Webb, 2006; Kelmshall, 2013), with more attention given to the years after 1990. I will then consider some of the legislative and policy changes affecting social work practice and education in a few international examples. As one (English) social worker/social work educator informant speaking in 2018 suggested to me: *"even though there are some key commonalities of social work across the world, I do think social work varies enormously from each country. So I don't necessarily think the challenges that are confronting social workers in the UK are necessarily the same challenges that are confronting social work elsewhere."*

Some of these changing legislative arrangements and policies affecting what we may think of as 'social work' will also illuminate what social work 'is' in different settings, and how social workers have responded to these different contexts, both in the UK (and its constituent countries) and elsewhere in Europe. Inevitably, I am selecting elements for this narrative that strike me as being significant from an outsider's perspective (and these will also relate more specifically to some issues in which I became more directly involved after 1990). For this reason, I should state that I am not choosing to focus only on 'English-speaking' countries as others may have done (on child protection, see, for example, Lonne et al, 2009). I cannot address in any depth social work in the US[1] or Australia,[2] which are both very significant environments in the development of social work but have been researched extensively elsewhere. This chapter will, I hope, both provide us with a background to later chapters and their more specific concerns, and give some indications for further reading.

Social welfare regimes internationally

To start off with a more general economic and political theme, broad commonalities have been identified internationally that relate to the nature of underpinning *social welfare regimes* and relevant social policies. As Cousins (2005) discusses, there are several different ways of theorising the origins of the 'welfare state' (for example, attributed to industrialisation, the needs of advanced capitalism, political and class struggles, or the structure and interests of the state). In their paper comparing social work in Britain, Australia and the US, McDonald, Harris and Wintersteen (2003: 195–6) suggest that:

> it is the social welfare regime that is the primary supporting institution for sustaining the project of social work ... [providing] social work with its legal and moral authority, as well as providing the actual physical conditions for practice. To varying degrees ... [social work is] the operational embodiment of modern welfare regimes.

'Social welfare regimes' vary between countries but have been amenable to grouping by 'ideal-type' (see Esping-Andersen, 1990), and these regimes have been discussed, for example, in relation to social work education in Europe (see Lyons, 2018). Writing in 1994, the influential Danish sociologist Esping-Andersen stated that:

> Since the early 1970s, we can identify three distinct welfare state responses to economic and social change. The Scandinavian countries followed, until recently, a strategy of welfare state-induced employment expansion in the public sector. The Anglo-Saxon countries – in particular Britain, New Zealand and the United States – have favoured a strategy of deregulating wages and the labour market, combined with a certain degree of welfare

state erosion. And the Continental European nations, like France, Germany or Italy, have favoured a strategy of induced labour supply reduction. All three strategies were intimately related to the nature of their welfare states. (Esping-Andersen, 1994)

Although influential, this typology has been critiqued, particularly for not taking geographical areas such as Southern Europe, Eastern Europe or Asia and their welfare systems more fully into account (see, for example, Ferrera, 1996; Kasza, 2002). In their recently edited collection focused on European welfare states, Blom, Evertsson and Perlinski, (2017), for example, follow an adapted, wider version of the overall (Esping-Andersen) framework, including examples not only from Nordic/Scandinavian countries and the UK, but also Eastern Europe (especially Poland). These kinds of examples can relate to the relationship between the state and social work or social work education (see, for example, Wódz and Falisek, 2017), as well as relationships with other sorts of organisations. Elsewhere, Kallio, Meeuwisse and Scaramuzzino (2016: 177) point out that a distinction between for-profit and non-profit organisations 'is often overlooked in welfare state research. Comparative welfare research usually assigns both these types of actors to the private sphere.' These authors developed a survey involving more than 8,000 respondents to compare social workers' attitudes towards privatisation in the Nordic countries (Denmark, Finland, Norway and Sweden) and Italy, thus representing two different models within the Esping-Andersen framework. They demonstrate that the picture is complicated by various issues, including individual factors and which type of organisation employed their social worker respondents. While 'privatisation' has occurred in all the countries in Kallio, Meeuwisse and Scaramuzzino's (2016) study, it seems that the Nordic countries still rely more on the public sector (though this is changing[3]), while in Italy, 'private' solutions (including the family) are more commonly used in dealing with social problems. Overall, these authors found that social workers' attitudes towards for-profit and non-profit privatisation are not the same; in their research, they were generally more positive about services in the 'non-profit' (voluntary sector) than the profit-making 'private' sector. For example, they found that 'Supporting increased citizens' involvement was more strongly connected to support for non-profit privatization ... than for for-profit privatization. This can be seen as consistent with the more participative characteristics of the non-profit sector compared to the for-profit sector' (Kallio et al, 2016: 190).

As illustrations from my own research, when I was speaking in 2018 to a social work educator in Denmark, I could begin to see how the underpinning but changing social welfare regime there can link to social work practice and social work education. This informant discussed how social work is organised and financed in Denmark, where the picture is also very complex:

Interviewer: '*So, when people leave your* [social work] *course, they would go to work where, where would they go to work?*'

Informant: '*It takes three-and-a-half years to become a social worker, a bachelor in social work* [in Denmark], *so after that, many of the educated go to the* [public sector] *municipalities, these areas. You know, social work as a profession is very associated with the welfare state, the way the welfare state is organised, so the municipalities are responsible for all that has to do with child welfare or, you know, employment services, disabilities, psychiatric, you know, social-psychiatric problems and things like that. You also have social workers employed in the region and in the state, for instance, in relation to criminality.*'

Interviewer: '*Criminality, yes.*'

Informant: '*Yes, or health social workers, if you work in hospitals, the regions are responsible for that.... You also have a lot of private institutions in Denmark for delivering services within child welfare, services for young people, homeless people, and you also have social workers employed there and then also in the community work area. So, it's a mixture of state-financed and also private, you know.*'

A recent interviewee working in England also commented to me on her view of the situation:

'*I, personally, am committed to social work being in the statutory or voluntary sector and I'm not sort of ideologically opposed to private-sector, you know, agencies, but I get concerned about ... a privatisation model. I mean, that's what's happening in health. It's a creeping concern that social care too could, there could be privatisation, because, for ideological reasons, some people think the market is everything.*' (Social worker/educator in England speaking in 2018)

Evolving policy and legislation in the UK in relation to social work

Returning to our historical background in the UK, Harris (2008), whose main interest is in the development of state-sponsored social work, and Dickens (2011), who compares 'watershed' moments relating to the Seebohm Report and the more recent Social Work Task Force (SWTF), both give us useful detail about the policy trajectories that have evolved over time in the UK. Harris (2008: 663) identifies five key 'historical moments' since the 19th century in the UK, where, he suggests, 'a particular discourse that proved to be significant for social work's development was in the ascendant in each of them'. Inevitably, there may be multiple discourses during each of these time periods, and over time, these moments are not simply discrete, but intertwined. I would agree with Harris that there can still be some present-day social policy ramifications for social work from these significant moments.[4] Together with Dickens's discussion, this framework has provided me with a useful starting point for a UK policy overview relevant to 'social work' since 1990, although I have amended both chronologies to cover recent developments in more detail, and especially those resulting from the Coalition and Conservative administrations since 2010.

Social work: a brief chronology of relevant policy and legislation in the UK

The 19th century

The 19th-century origins of social work were characterised by the work of the Charity Organisation Society, providing interventions in the lives of the 'working-class poor'. Important legislation in this period included the 1834 Poor Law and the Public Health Acts in 1848 and 1872. There are continuing debates about the relevance of moral and religious influences on social work development that began at this time (see, for example, Bowpitt, 1998).

Early 20th century

In this period, various Acts of Parliament introduced 'old-age' pensions (in 1908) and the school medical service (in 1907), while the National Insurance Act 1911 addressed medical care and unemployment. The Local Government Act 1929 transferred the management of publicly funded hospitals to local authorities, which had many responsibilities by the 1930s, for example, education, health and social assistance. Some social work historians (see, for example, Burnham, 2011) have recently indicated that a *public sector legacy* dating from before the First World War contributed to the later development of social work (after 1948); however, Burnham also suggests that this has not been fully recognised.

Development of the post-war welfare state

Following the 1942 Beveridge Report, which identified five 'giants' blocking post-war reconstruction ('disease, ignorance, squalor, idleness and want'), Harris (2008:669) suggests that the key significance for social work was in 'its incorporation into a niche in the welfare state, with legal powers and aspirations for a generic method in psycho-dynamic casework, and its having a place in the delivery of social citizenship'.

The 1960s and 1970s: changes to professional identity and service structures

The 1968 Seebohm Report recommended changes in the personal social services, including a greater focus on *universalism* in service provision. Social work's professional identity and the service structure were merged. According to Harris (2008: 671), 'Social workers were to be neither autonomous professionals nor bureaucratic functionaries; social work was to exist in its own right, within the shell of local government administration, as a form of bureau-professionalism.'

Following the Seebohm recommendations, this was the era that saw the setting up of local authority social services departments (in 1971). The British Association of Social Workers (BASW) was also established in 1970 with the amalgamation of seven social work-related organisations (for more details, see, for example, Payne, 2002; Dickens, 2011; University of Warwick, 2012). There were developments in social work education at this time, with the national (and renamed) Central Council for Education and Training in Social Work (CCETSW) being established in 1971 (the previous Council for Training in Social Work had been established in 1962).

CCETSW (which was divided into regions, including the London and South-East region) took over the training functions of some social work professional associations, and launched the Certificate of Qualification in Social Work (CQSW), a generic social work qualification, in 1972 (see also Dickens, 2011: 28); this was followed by the Certificate in Social Service (CSS) qualification (mainly attracting residential workers) in 1975. As described by the University of Warwick's Modern Records Centre archives, CCETSW was 'a UK-wide, statutory organisation responsible for promoting, approving and assuring the quality of education and training for social work and social care staff in the personal social services' (University of Warwick, 2012).

The 1980s onwards: new managerialism, marketisation and performativity

The development of quasi-markets, the introduction of a 'purchaser–provider split' in welfare and the use of the contracting out of services all occurred during this time. Harris indicates that the main discursive shift that occurred under the Thatcher and Major governments during this period involved *examining the effects and costs of welfare*, as well as an overall *rolling back of the state*. During this time, the Barclay Report (1982: 198) considered social workers' roles and tasks, and recommended a decentralisation of social services; it emphasised that a key role for the personal social services was to 'develop a close working partnership with citizens focusing more closely on the community and its strengths' (p 198). Social workers would then be able to motivate others to care. Our third informant in Chapter 1 also recalled (approvingly) an era when "*Back then* [early 1990s], *social work services were located in the communities they were serving.*"

Following Esping-Anderson, Chandler et al (2015: 109) describe how trends of 'marketization and differentiation on the one hand and managerialization and performativity on the other' came, over time, to affect social work in both the UK and in other countries (including Sweden) as a result of neoliberal policies. The implications of this development of neoliberalism are also reflected in the comments made by some of my earlier informants quoted in Chapter 1. Others have also discussed more generally the wider effects of what became known as the 'New Public Management' (NPM) (see, for example, McLaughlin et al, 2001).[5]

From the 1980s onwards, a separate legislative emphasis focused on children and on vulnerable adults, and includes the following key measures that were fundamental to the transformation of social work:

• The Children Act (which remains a key legislative milestone) was published in 1989, with its subsequent amendments, including the 2004 Act.

- The Mental Health Act 1983 (later amended in 2007).
- The NHS and Community Care Act 1990, relating to reforms affecting adult 'Care in the Community', with the legislative sequence involving, first, the original Griffiths Report (1988),[6] then the subsequent White Paper (in 1989) and then the Act itself (implemented in 1993.
- Also at this time, in 1991, *social work education* in the UK changed from being based on the official dual qualifications of CSS and CQSW to the single, two-year Diploma in Social Work (DipSW).

Later 1990s: 'modernising social services' and New Labour

With the advent of the New Labour government in the UK in 1997, there were a number of ideological shifts affecting social welfare and social work, although a continued reliance on 'managerialism' was still evident. Harris (2008: 675) suggests that this was different from the Conservative perspective because New Labour's managerialism 'was presented as empowering everyone.... [It] purported to speak for service users and any resistance to managerialism by social workers was attacked as simply elitist professional attempts to avoid accountability to users'. Harris suggests that since local authorities had already been weakened during the period of Thatcherism, this enabled New Labour to continue to develop a 'mixed economy of welfare', pursuing managerialist goals. Initiatives of relevance to social work during the New Labour administration included the development of 'Sure Start' (established in 1998) relating to childcare, health, family support and early education. The Social Care Institute for Excellence (SCIE), which continues as an independent charity providing knowledge and education/training materials, was also established in 2001.

UK government aims at this time to 'modernise' social services (Department of Health, 1998) and to provide a 'quality strategy' for social care set out to enable national standards to be pursued at local level, with the overall aim of raising those standards (see Department of Health, 2000a). The government created what Dickens (2011: 33) has referred to as 'an elaborate network of new agencies in its drive to "modernise" social services'. As a specific example of contemporary legislation, in 2000, a White Paper on adoption was published (see Department of Health, 2000b), followed by the Adoption and Children Act 2002, which reformed the legislation in this area and brought it into line with the earlier Children Act. Under this legislation, the greater use of adoption was encouraged, and where parents did not agree to the adoption of their child, this matter was to be settled by the courts in the best interests of the child.[7]

These various attempts at the reform of social work and welfare were not without critics, who have suggested that, overall, there were 'muddles, inconsistencies and gaps' in the government's programme, which also led to 'damaging unintended consequences' (Jordan, 2000: 1). Political devolution into the *four countries of the UK* in the late 1990s (Wales and Northern Ireland each having their own national Assembly and Scotland its own Parliament) meant that the governance of social work became focused more specifically on those separate 'country' administrations. It should be noted that there are increasing differences in legislation and social work practice between these four UK countries:

> [Child protection] policy is a devolved power and increasing differences of approach are being seen between the countries.... Scotland has an entirely separate legal system to that in England and Wales with different terminology and structures. The Scottish children's hearings system is unique ... children's services in Northern Ireland [are] being managed through joint Health and Social Care Trusts rather than by elected local councils as in the three other countries. (Bywaters et al, 2018: 5)

CCETSW was disbanded as a UK-wide organisation in September 2001 and many of its functions passed to the four new care councils: the General Social Care Council (GSCC) for England; the Scottish Social Services Council (SSSC); the Care Council for Wales (CCW); and the Northern Ireland Social Care Council (NISCC). In the same year, the UK government announced further radical changes to social work education, resulting in the replacement of the existing DipSW by a three-year degree from 2003. Following this change in England, similar changes (to a minimum of a degree-level education) were made in Scotland, Wales and Northern Ireland (see Department of Health, 2001; Orme et al, 2009).

Payne (writing in 2002), a founder member of the BASW in 1970, provides a useful and detailed discussion of the developments associated with that organisation, and especially BASW's links to other 'stakeholders' relevant to social work. BASW had also supported the change from a two-year diploma to a three-year degree in social work. However, the role of this (membership) organisation, despite its longevity (operating since 1970), has sometimes found itself subject to criticism, particularly in terms of its 'limited impact' in the context of later developments (see later; see also Dickens, 2011: 35).

Towards the end of the Labour administrations (in 2010), the SWTF was set up (in November 2008) in order to address what were perceived at that time by the government and others from within and outside the profession as necessary social work reforms. Dickens (2011) suggests that a dominant force shaping social policy and practice in England from the 1970s onwards was concern about how social workers responded to cases of child abuse. In this, he concurs with Stevenson (writing in 2005), who dates this 'moral panic', and the start of an 'era of child protection enquiries', to 1973/74 and the 1974 report of an enquiry into the death of Maria Colwell, a child who had been killed by her step-father. Stevenson (2005: 578) comments that the 1974 enquiry report 'marked the beginning of a new phase in the relationships between the public and social work, with the media as a critical intervening force'. Dickens (2011: 30) suggests that the SWTF's 'immediate origins lay in the outrage and distress caused by the most recent child abuse scandal in England'.

Members of the SWTF (including senior figures involved in social work and social services, third sector organisations, service user groups, academia, and the media) produced interim reports and then a final report in 2009, which made 15 key recommendations, including the establishment of a National College of Social Work to provide 'greater leadership' for the profession. Dickens notes a change of tone across these SWTF reports, moving from an initial focus on the heavy workloads confronting social workers to a final emphasis on 'selecting the right sort of people and training them to cope with these heavy demands, and much less on alleviating the intolerable pressures' (Dickens, 2011: 31).

From 2010 to the present day: austerity and after – the Coalition and subsequent Conservative administration(s)

With UK government changes from 2010 (the Coalition government) and from 2015 (Conservative administrations), there came further important changes to welfare legislation and policy in the UK. This coincided with difficult global economic problems from 2008 onwards, resulting in a period of what commentators have called *austerity*, with severe reductions in UK public sector funding as well as continuation of the *rolling back of the state*, as in earlier decades. In terms of social work, this policy trajectory has had, and continues to have, a profound impact (see, for example, Garrett, 2014).

In addition to policy reports and further legislation, this time period has involved a number of upheavals relating to the governance of social work as a profession (including social work education) in the UK, which I next indicate briefly ; I will discuss these issues further later in the book (for example, in relation to education [Chapters 4 and 5] and state involvement with social work [Chapter 10]).

The SWTF led into the Social Work Reform Board (SWRB), which was set up in 2010 and presented its final progress report in June 2012 (SWRB, 2012). A key policy development at this time was also the review of child protection by Professor Eileen Munro, who reported in 2011 (Munro, 2011). Among her recommendations, key issues were to provide a reduction in bureaucracy and a child protection system that places more emphasis on valuing professional social work expertise. Specific recommendations (of which there were 15) included:

- a central place for 'the child's journey' (from needing to receiving help) and looking at the effectiveness of that help;
- removing unnecessary bureaucracy, especially unhelpful targets for completing assessments within a set timescale;
- including all local services (that is, not only social work) involved in the protection of children during inspections;
- changes to the ways in which serious case reviews are conducted; and
- local authorities to designate a Principal Child and Family Social Worker and the government to appoint a Chief Social Worker to advise on social work practice and inform the annual report to Parliament on the working of the Children Act 1989.

The Munro review was widely welcomed, including reportedly by the Children's Commissioner for England and the British Association for Adoption and Fostering (now Coram BAAF). By June 2012, the SWRB's final progress report stated that progress in social work reform since 2010 had included the establishment of The College of Social Work (TCSW) in 2012 as a subscription-based organisation, and ongoing recruitment for the post of Chief Social Worker for England. In the event, two (continuing) posts were designated: the Chief Social Worker for Children and Families; and the Chief Social Worker for Adults. The SWRB's Professional Capabilities Framework (PCF) was also produced in 2012 as an overarching requirement for all social workers in England, wherever they are employed (including those working independently).[8] Also in 2012, the renamed Health and

Care Professions Council (HCPC) took over from the GSCC as the regulator for social work professionals in England.

After the Munro review, an All Party Parliamentary Group on Social Work was launched in January 2012 following lobbying from BASW. A report was produced in 2013 by the group (in association with BASW), which made several recommendations and aimed to ensure that 'the profession can see the impact of previous reforms [particularly coming from the SWTF, SWRB and Munro review] and retain a belief that strongly identified concerns, and prescriptions for improvement, are followed through with real change' (All Party Parliamentary Group on Social Work, 2013: 8). In 2015, in what was widely described as a 'shock' development, TCSW collapsed following the withdrawal of government financial support; debates have continued about the causes and implications of this demise (for reactions from the social work profession and others, see, for example, Brindle, 2015; McNicoll, 2016; for further discussion, see also Chapter 10, this volume).

Notable legislation since 2014 relevant to social work in England includes the following:

- The Care Act 2014 (implemented in 2015): this Act reformed the law relating to care and support for adults and support for carers. It addressed the safeguarding of adults from abuse or neglect, as well as care standards. The Act also established Health Education England and the Health Research Authority. It made provisions relating to the integration of care and support with health services.
- The Children and Families Act 2014: this wide-ranging Act addressed further reforms for the adoption system, for example, by repealing requirements for local authorities to give 'due consideration' to children's ethnic, religious, cultural or linguistic backgrounds when matching them with adopters. It also addressed the needs of children in care and those with special educational needs.
- The Children and Social Work Act 2017: this Act relates to looked-after children and child safeguarding, and establishes a new regulatory body, Social Work England (to replace the HCPC[9] in future).

Some key legislation and policies relevant to social work in European countries

In the next section, I will briefly address relevant policies and legislation in a few example European countries, particularly:

- Sweden
- Denmark
- Portugal
- Romania
- Switzerland

I chose these countries to reflect different types of welfare regime, as discussed earlier, as well as because they are places where I have had some personal contacts or have been able to obtain information to support research for this book. As Lyons (2018: 3), referencing Lorenz, notes: 'Europe is "not a fixed entity" but rather "a project".' This also means that I feel more comfortable with making a limited selection of countries for my own purposes. Direct quotes from my interviews with social workers and social work educators in this section are placed in *italics*. Apart from Switzerland, all the other countries that I have chosen are currently members of the European Union (EU) and the European Economic Area (EEA).

The EU introduced a directive[10] on the recognition of professional qualifications (including for social work) that came into effect in 2007: 'setting out the procedures, which national governments must adhere to when assessing the qualifications of a trained social worker from another EEA country' (Hussein, 2014: i181). Hussein's (2014: i183) research with 'transnational' social workers (TSWs) also reports that most social workers coming to the UK from the EEA felt 'an overwhelming level of difference between social work practice in the UK and their home countries'. (I include some material on the experiences of a few TSWs that I have interviewed in various chapters of this book [see also Hanna and Lyons, 2017].)

Denmark and Sweden

Both these Nordic countries broadly fall within what has been termed by Esping-Andersen and others as the 'social-democratic' type of welfare regime (in relation to Denmark, see also Torfing, 1999). In Sweden, social work and the personal social services currently remain largely within the public sector and are governed by the Social Services Act 2001. The public sector in Sweden is divided into the national state, county and local municipal levels. Since 1992, the Local Government Act 1991 has provided the 290 municipalities with some freedom to organise their services differently, but within a tripartite framework, involving political decisions (setting goals and deciding budgets), administrative and managerial arrangements, and professionals working directly with clients/service users (see, for example, Perlinski et al, 2012). However, as Chandler et al (2015: 110) suggest, 'legislative change [in Sweden] has opened up opportunities for local authorities to subcontract services to private entrepreneurs and third sector organisations'.

There has reportedly been greater specialisation into different areas of social work in Sweden in recent years (Perlinski et al, 2012), although this approach may be seen as inadequate when dealing with complex social problems (Blom, 2004). There has been no 'protected title' for social workers in Sweden until recently (as linked to the registration of social workers in the UK); however, I understand that new legislation in 2019 will introduce this for social workers in the health sector. Trade unions and the municipalities may arguably play more of a role in defining the occupation/profession (see Chandler et al, 2015); however, social work education is regulated in Sweden (Hussein, 2014: i181).

Like other Nordic countries, Denmark has a long history of welfare legislation; the first Danish child protection legislation dates from 1905, influenced by earlier Norwegian legislation. Currently, there is emphasis in relation to family welfare on ensuring the child's best interests, as reflected in the United Nations Convention on the Rights of the Child. The Danish Social Service Law (*Lov om social service*) originally dates from 1998 and is regularly updated. Child protection services in Denmark include a focus on abuse and neglect; the 2013 '*Overgrebspakke*' (package relating to abuse) was integrated into the Law on Social Service, in which there is generally a focus on the child's well-being and development, and the provision of family- and child-oriented services. The current version of the Law on Social Service is from 2018[11] (see also Poso et al, 2014). As in Sweden (see earlier), there is a focus on the 98 local municipalities assessing the needs for social services of children and their families, young people, and adults with special support needs. There is an increasing specialisation of welfare services, although the education of social workers remains generic. During an interview with me in 2018, the following social work educator stated:

> '*we had a huge reform in 2007 where the municipalities got the overall responsibility for delivering social services and the complexity of the tasks and also the, kind of, the whole volume of different services just increased a lot ... social workers today are much more identifying with the kind of people that they are working with and the specific context that they're in. And it's also a political context,*

you know, in Denmark, it's, you have social policies for all kinds
of areas and it's highly regulated by law as well.'

An interesting aspect of social work in Denmark (as well as in Sweden, Germany and Finland) is that while some people (identifying as 'social workers') are educated with a BA in social work (as we saw earlier in this chapter), others train as 'pedagogues'/'social pedagogues' (with a BA degree) (see Eriksson, 2014; Bain and Evans, 2017).[12] In Denmark, the 'profession-BA'[13] in social work is mainly provided by university colleges; Aalborg University also provides this course, as well as a social work master's programme. 'Social pedagogues' may work in similar areas to social workers, for example, in residential care (see also Cameron, 2004); however, there are differences in what these occupations are taught during their education. Social workers are educated in legal methods and legislation much more than pedagogues, and this has to do with their position in the municipalities, doing statutory social work. There is thus some ambiguity about the tasks relevant to those working in these two occupations. As a profession, 'social work' does not currently have a 'protected title' in Denmark.

Portugal

Ferrera (1996) describes Portugal as belonging to a 'Southern model' of welfare (along with Spain, Greece and Italy). This model is very broadly characterised by institutional fragmentation (though this reportedly occurs less in Portugal than elsewhere in the 'Southern' regimes), as well as by having an important role for cash benefits (especially pensions) alongside universalism in health-care provision. At the time Ferrera was writing, Portugal had relatively lower incomes and one of the higher rates of poor households in the EU. Meanwhile, Branco (2018), in a discussion of the history of social work education in Portugal, describes how the first school of social work was established in Lisbon in 1935, and that social work education was first regulated in 1939. Male students were only admitted to the profession from 1961/62.

Since the revolution of 1974 and the subsequent 1976 Constitution, children's rights to protection have been recognised by the state; in 1990, Portugal ratified the United Nations Convention on the Rights of the Child. Key legislation relevant to social work with families and children includes the 1999 Law of Protection of Children and Young People at Risk (Law 147/99), which was later revised by Law 142/2015 (Portugal, 2015). This law 'regulates the State's intervention in the promotion and protection of the rights of children in situations of risk when the parents, or legal representative or factual guardian places at risk the safety, health, education and development of the child' (see CESIS, 2017: 3). Local Committees for Protection of Children and Young People (CPCJs) are organised on a municipal basis and work in partnership with different groups in the local community, including health and education services and non-governmental organisations (NGOs) (in Portugal, these are referred to as non-profit private social solidarity institutions [IPSSs]) (CESIS, 2017: 6; see also Ferreira, 2005).

For older citizens, 'social work operates within the Department of Social Security, by helping older people claiming welfare benefits and by managing residential and domiciliary care services for the ageing population' (Carvalho, 2014: 340). Local authorities now also have partnerships with the health service and the voluntary sector 'to ensure that older people's issues are reflected strategically in local plans and strategies. Some local authorities promote an active participation of older people in the decision-making processes through local forums' (Carvalho, 2014: 342).

These recent changes and the increasing bureaucratisation of social work activities were discussed by a Portuguese social worker in her recent interview; she explained to me that she had qualified in social work in 1998 after a five-year course, before the introduction of the three- or three-and-a-half-year degree relating to the standardising Bologna Process in Europe (see Labonté-Roset, 2004). At that time (in 1998), "*most* [Portuguese] *social workers were employed by the state and with more or less formal jobs, structured jobs, a career ... and now it's not the case anymore because there was a very strong movement of the state transferring responsibilities into the third sector*" (social worker/social work educator speaking in 2018). Social work education has also developed since that time and has become well established in universities over the past decade (including, for example, University Institute of Lisbon [ISCTE-IUL]).

Romania

Romania has experienced several stages in the 20th-century development of social work. Social work developed following the First World War (when Romania was created as a nation-state in 1918), and a school of social work was established in 1929. According to Lazăr (2015: 68), 'In 1943 a new law organized the social assistance activity within the Ministry of Labor, health and social welfare in three departments: social assistance, family protection and mother and child protection.' After the Second World War, with the arrival of the communist regime, there were reorganisations at the government level and 'attempts to reduce the role of social work, mainly for ideological reasons' (Lazăr, 2015: 68); people were 'expected to be equal' and so social workers had a marginal role. Lazăr describes how civil servants replaced social workers as the well developed social work system was gradually 'dismantled, reorganised and responsibilities divided between various departments and ministers. The dissolution of social work education (at university level in 1952 and completely in 1969) was the final step in demolishing the profession' (Lazăr, 2015: 69).

The revolution of 1989 and the fall of communism resulted in further changes and a resurgence of social work education from 1990 onwards. Since then, there have been many developments, especially in the child protection field (Cojocaru, 2008). Many international NGOs initially responded to the well-publicised welfare needs of children in residential care since there were few recently trained social workers in Romania in the early 1990s. Reforms to child protection began in 1997, and in the early 2000s, further legislation was enacted relating to social assistance and cash benefits. A National College of Social Workers was established in 2005, which is the central organisation currently regulating the profession; by 2013, about 4,500 social workers in Romania were registered with the National College, rising to about 8,000 currently. A code of ethics for social work was also established in 2008: "*The College is the professional body which is consulted by ministries and others, in drafting legislation. Usually, it's consulted on issues around social workers and social professions*" (social worker/educator speaking in 2018).

With the accession of Romania to the EU in 2007, and in the years leading up to this change, support from Europe required the Romanian government to reshape its social policies (Lazăr et al, 2019). The World Bank also became an important influence from the mid-1990s, and especially since the financial crash in 2008, resulting in the development of austerity and neoliberal political and policy agendas across Europe. Major changes in the social assistance system in Romania are being developed with the World Bank's support as part of the *National strategy on social inclusion and poverty reduction 2015–2020* (see Lazăr et al, 2019). A majority of social workers in Romania reportedly work in child protection. There are developments in the privatisation of some social work services and the National College now permits those with more than five years' practice experience to establish themselves in private practice (though this can lead to an uneven distribution of services, especially where this tends to happen in more urban areas (Lazăr et al, 2019: 4).

In terms of social work education, there remains a shortfall in the number of qualified social workers in Romania but steps are being taken to address this. According to the view of the following social worker and social work educator whom I interviewed in 2018:

> *'recently, two or three years ago I think, there were some regulations introduced which say that in order to be able to provide social work services or social services, you need to have qualified social workers employed. So, you cannot get accredited … and this is a big step because, in this way, people, for instance NGOs, but also public agencies, are forced to employ qualified social workers.'*

Switzerland

Switzerland has a federal structure in which 'the twenty-six Cantons have a high degree of self-governance which makes implementation of any national policy a complex undertaking' (Spratt et al, 2015: 1515). The population is also divided into four language groups (French, German, Italian and Romansh), with more than half of them speaking German. This means that 'policy development at the federal level involves building a consensus across the different cultural norms and perspectives represented by Canton governments' (Spratt et al, 2015: 1515). Federal legislation must therefore be acceptable in principle to all cultures yet flexible enough to be implemented at the canton level. The Swiss constitution 'guarantees a right to social assistance; it cannot be denied except in cases of fraud, or of refusal to provide the requested documentation. It is implemented differently in each canton' (Tabin and Perriard, 2016: 433). Tabin et al (2011: 475) point out that:

> social workers working for authorities in Switzerland have to deal with laws resting upon different ways of conceiving of social solidarity. As a consequence, they are confronted with moral dilemmas when working with asylum seekers or undocumented migrants … [and] they have to refuse help to people who need it in a State which claims that only dignity matters.

A Swiss social worker whom I interviewed in 2018 explained to me that, as in some other countries in Europe, social workers have a wide remit, including dealing with financial benefits: "*social services [in Switzerland] are responsible … for the kind of personal social services, but also for the benefit side. So, social services are paying out the sustenance, if you like, the financial support, housing benefit, everything goes through social services."* Switzerland's long-established child protection law was revised in 2013, with the child protection service being professionalised; this service was made independent from political authorities. (These revisions followed an international project relating to comparative child protection practices commissioned by the Swiss federal government [for details, see Spratt et al, 2015].)

As described in Article 3.1 (a) of the European Directive, 'social worker' is not a protected title in Switzerland. Social workers are not required to register with a regulatory body as there is 'no recognised social work professional body in Switzerland' (Hussein, 2011: 67). However, social work education generally follows the 'Bologna Process' pattern seen elsewhere, with a three-year bachelor's degree as the main qualification (see Labonté-Roset, 2004). In Switzerland, a generic qualification would include social work, social pedagogy and youth and community work, and allow graduates to work in a variety of settings. In the next chapter, we will consider how and why people decide to train as social workers and we can begin to look in more depth at how social work education and training has evolved since 1990.

Chapter 3 summary

In this chapter, I have given a brief contextual background history to 'social work', emphasising the years after 1990, since when there have been many policy and political changes and theoretical developments in the UK and internationally affecting social work practice and education. This is the time period during which I have had my own involvement with social workers and social work education. I chose some comparative geographical locations partly to reflect aspects of my own involvement with social work and contacts with social work and social workers in those places, as well as to reflect different kinds of welfare regime (as identified by Esping-Andersen) and to indicate some different kinds of welfare professional, as discussed in the first part of the chapter.

Notes

[1] For discussions of the history of social work in the US, see, for example, Ehrenreich (2014), Popple (2018) and Reisch and Andrews (2002).

[2] For discussions of social work in Australia, see Mendes (2005), Maidment and Bay (2012) and the journal Australian Social Work.

[3] For further comparisons between England and Sweden, see also Chandler et al (2015).

[4] Other useful historical summaries about social work in addition to those produced by Harris and Dickens include books by Bamford (2015) and Pierson (2011). A 'centenary timeline' covering historical events and those relevant to social work and social work education is also available on the University of Edinburgh website (see: www.socialwork.ed.ac.uk/centenary/timeline).

[5] These effects are said to include processes of de-professionalisation. For relevant links to anthropology, see also Strathern (2000) and Shore and Wright (2015).

[6] Interestingly, Whittington (1998: 97) notes that while social work 'was at the centre of many of the Seebohm proposals ... Griffiths had barely mentioned it at all'.

[7] This legislation has had implications for the support offered to birth parents whose children are taken into care and/or adopted (though the possibility of such parental support was referred to in this Act) (see, for example, Lewis-Brooke et al, 2017).

[8] Social workers in Wales, Northern Ireland or Scotland continue to use the existing National Occupational Standards for Social Work.

[9] For HCPC statistics about social work 'registrants' at the time of writing this book (in June 2018), see Chapter 7.

[10] Directive 2005/36/EC.

[11] See: www.retsinformation.dk/forms/R0710.aspx?id=202239

[12] Bain and Evans (2017) report that German-trained social pedagogues recruited as social workers in England continued to see themselves as social pedagogues while adapting to English statutory social work.

[13] This is legally different from a 'regular' BA, for example, in sociology.

4

Becoming: being admitted, educated and trained in social work

Introduction

Why do people become social workers? What motivates them to take up this occupation? Furthermore, who should be accepted by others as a social worker? As we have already seen in Chapter 3, the legislative and policy contexts that provide a background to social work in the UK (England, Wales, Scotland and Northern Ireland), as well as in a few selected European countries, are very complex. We have already seen that in Europe, other occupations such as social pedagogy are closely linked to social work; in some ways, as this book progresses, I feel that I am considering a complex set of welfare/caring occupations and not just one profession (see also Lyons, 2018[1]; Pawlas-Czyz et al, 2017[2]). These occupations all seem to be tied into the ethical and practical underpinnings related to compassion and social justice that we have already identified.

Chapter 3 also raised the whole issue of the interdependence of social work with the state and within changing policy contexts. The UK is relatively unusual in having a specific protected title of 'social worker', while those in similar occupations elsewhere, including social pedagogues, may carry out similar tasks. Furthermore, as we have already seen, social work tasks are extended in some parts of Europe, for example, to include responsibility for financial benefits. However, underpinning all of this variety is the need to somehow educate people into these welfare roles, and to allow them to (collaboratively) construct their professional identities (see Chapters 5 and 6; see also Bell et al, 2017).

Clark (2006: 87–8) is very clear that 'It is right ... to attend to the [moral] character, as well as the technical skill, of individuals who wish to work as professionals in the human services.' This immediately raises issues of *ethics* and *responsibility*, which, as we noted in Chapter 1, means that for most social workers, social work cannot be just a job; it is likely to be something that underpins their sense of *identity*. Ethical underpinnings to social work education, involving reflection about personal motivation and positive use of life experiences (including 'turning bad experiences into good' [see Dillon, 2011]), have therefore been clearly identified as relevant by social workers themselves (see, for example, Hafford-Letchfield and Dillon, 2015). These themes – of *ethics*, *values* and *identity* – will be discussed further in Chapters 6 and 7 (see also Holmström, 2014).

In this chapter, I am first going to explore in more detail the idea of the motivation to become a social worker, and what some key informants have said about this. Then, I will begin to consider two themes: 'What do social workers need to know?' and, more broadly, 'How has social work education been organised and structured?' I will focus in this chapter on what the state, including official regulator(s), think social workers should know and how this should be organised. In Chapter 5 ('Growing'), we go on to consider experiences of education and training in more detail. As before, I am attempting to look at these issues through fresh eyes, almost as if we could start by knowing nothing about these processes. But having been involved with social work education for many years now, it is surprisingly difficult to shed the assumptions (and language), coming from different perspectives, that I have become accustomed to during this time. This process of exploring education and training is made more complicated by the many and sometimes rapid changes in structure and policies that I and my social work colleagues have experienced over the past 20 years or so (as noted in Chapter 3).

Motivation: why social work?

Research with social work students taking the three-year degree in England (Stevens et al, 2010), supported by earlier investigations, has suggested that the motivation to become a social worker is enduring over time. Stevens et al (2010: 33) state that 'Altruistic motivations, often influenced by personal experiences, are the most important with a slight tendency towards more individualistic rather than collectivist altruism.' From my own interviews with a much smaller number of informants, I would concur that through all the changes to social work education and training, the imperative to do something to alleviate social problems and to act on these feelings of compassion seems to remain for aspiring social workers. Learning to become a social worker happens formally at the initial (or, what is called in the UK, 'qualifying' level) of higher or further education, but it can also start informally before that in various ways, including from very personal experiences, as the following informants explained in their interviews with me:

'I'd done community work and had, you know, managed to transition into social work by building up a little portfolio for myself of experience. Although I was very young when I went into it, I was probably one of the youngest people on the course, but I still wanted to do that because I wanted to know that it was something that I could do and wanted to go into.' (Social worker/social work educator who qualified in the 1980s, interviewed in 2018)

'I qualified around 2007/08 as a social worker. Prior to that, I worked within domestic violence and trafficking, and managed a refuge, and mainly my involvement was [overseas]. *I came here* [UK] *to complete my master's in social work.... I come from a country* [US] *where there is a very clear route that you only are a social worker if you have a master's minimum and that you cannot have a PGDip or a BA or anything.'* (Transnational[3] social worker now in the UK, interviewed in 2018)

'I had an accident and I was in a coma for several days. Nobody [expected] *... that I will return to life ... so I wanted to live again. So, after that, I had one or two years because I lost my mind, I don't remember anything ... but I was starting my new life again. And in those days, I learned ... the problem with refugees in the world.* [They] *make me think that I don't want to be a creative director any more. So, I want to study anything that I can learn and more information about what's happening in the world for so many refugees.... I decided to study social work because I think it was the most, it was the course that indicated to myself how I can learn more about people because I changed my life after the accident. Before I just was a workaholic absolutely, 24 hours a day. After my accident, I looked to the people and I feel much more the presence of each* [person] *and the love that I can give to them and the help I can give to them. I changed my life and I feel much more energy and power in each person. So, I want to be near people and listen to them because millions of people want to speak and nobody listens to them. It is happening in all the world.... So, I decided to learn how I can be with people and I can give some of myself and receive what they want to give me. And that's the reason I chose social work, to be near people.'* (Recently qualified social worker, studying in Europe, interviewed in 2018)

While some of my informants explained these informal, personal experiences that led them into a career in social work, others (like the next informant) said that they had previously trained for a different career that may nevertheless have had caring elements that prompted the move into social work, as in this case:

'*My motivation to consider social work pre-empts my arrival in the UK because I was working in substance misuse* [as a mental health nurse] *and, yes, I was exposed to, in my view, very good social workers, who made me realise that actually all those things that I thought I should be doing as a nurse* [such as working holistically], *as a social worker, they were able to do....*

So, that started the whole process, why I did my certificate in social work, which isn't recognised in the UK, or even in my own country, because ... it's vocational training, because it's done part time, it's not professional training. So, coming to the UK, I had the opportunity because, at the time, the policy in mental health was to train what they call generic mental health workers. I was kind of lucky, I was in the right place at the right time and I was able to lay my cards on the table, as it were, and I ended up the only person in that [health] *trust who actually wanted to make that change and go and study social work. So, I was trained by the NHS* [National Health Service] *to become a social worker. The irony of it all is when I finished training as a social worker, they didn't want to know I even existed! I was told quite plainly by my manager "If you want to do social work, then you'll have to leave the NHS and go and work in the local authority."'* (Transnational social worker, dual qualified in mental health nursing and social work, interviewed in 2018)

This next informant also pursued both nursing and social work:

'*I would say I fell into both careers.... I trained to be a nurse* [in the 1980s]. *I did that for a couple of years, but I always had this desire that I wanted to go to university, and so I went to see the careers officer because I had been working as a, I had qualified as a nurse for about two years and I really wanted to go to university. So, the careers officer said "Oh, there's ...", and I said I want to do a degree that will give me a job at the end, so he said "Oh, there's a space at the university for social work, why don't you, what about that?" And I didn't know anything about it whatsoever, all I remembered was what the social workers did at the hospital and I thought "Oh, that looks very interesting and nice." So, I had no idea of what social work was, but I wanted to do a social science degree at the same time, just like a combined course. So, I ended up going onto a social work course.'* (Dual-qualified nurse/social worker, interviewed in 2018)

The quotes from these last two interviews illustrate how (and why) these informants got into social work instead of continuing with their previous career; however, these processes were complicated rather than straightforward, as both these informants suggest. These two informants acknowledged that they brought with them elements of their previous education and work experience in nursing, which included being familiar with the language around health and being able to work with other professionals; in the case of the first informant, there came continuing specialisation in mental health social work, albeit outside the NHS.

While I was teaching about research and research methods mainly to professional students in health care, nursing, mental health and social work, during my years as a university lecturer, I was often asked to participate in admissions events or to interview prospective students for places on social work undergraduate or postgraduate programmes. I think that, overall, it was assumed that admission to professional programmes at university level meant that we would be assessing people for suitability for the profession or occupation and not only for their admission to the course itself. Yet, my outsider position as a non-professional did not seem to be a barrier to getting involved in social work admissions; I was always careful to try and work alongside qualified social work educators, which felt more comfortable and not to be overstepping the professional mark. However, in more recent years, and especially since social work in the UK acquired its protected title, I did notice that my attempts to work in this way were perhaps taken more seriously, which I am sure is not a coincidence. (Interestingly I was never asked to interview prospective undergraduate nursing students, though I did teach them research methods.)

The following auto-ethnographic account of a student recruitment day gives a flavour of my experiences with university admissions (student recruitment) to social work, and may also shed some further light on who was applying to study social work at my university after the new three-year social work degree was established from 2003 onwards. (For wider discussion on this topic of admissions to social work education, see also Moriarty and Murray, 2007[4]; Holmström, 2010.)

A recruitment day: auto-ethnographic observations

I arrive at the campus just after 9.30am to find the event in full swing. Various staff are sitting at their allocated desks with large signs proclaiming our subject areas, grouped by school. In our school section, I find my colleague, O, who is a fellow lecturer. A neat sign on the desk in university colours gives our names and job titles.

Confusion had already reigned this week when I tried to find out definitively whether or not we were needed today. It seems that there are two simultaneous events going on (very confusingly): an admissions day for social work students (interviewing current-year applicants), which had been de facto cancelled (as one had already been held during the previous week); and an open day for prospective university candidates (for next year), at which two social work representatives were required.

I am still not sure which of these events I had been signed up for (but probably for both). The admissions tutor (not here today) had claimed knowledge of the first event but not the second. I knew the social work department had been in touch with today's organisers (who were, in fact, managing both events). Now that I am well established in my department, I tend to (loyally) view my usual experience of recruitment days as involving well-organised social work colleagues grappling valiantly with university systems. The chief social work lecturer had contacted me yesterday to say that I needed to find a replacement for myself if I was not attending today (thereby putting me in the position of having to replace that person on another occasion). I decided that it was easier to give up my Saturday and attend.

O is pleased to see me and I briefly explain to her what has been happening this week. I check that she is willing to give the social work talk as required as I have no clue about the current arrangements for BA students (apparently the main focus of today). I say that this is because I tend to mainly work with postgraduate and research students and, unlike me, O is a qualified social worker.[5] She says that there is an online presentation on the collective staff website that they used before, so she will use that. We are informed by the university open day organisers that 34 people have signed up in advance to find out more about social work; this is probably the largest group showing an interest in any specific degree programme for the whole university, except perhaps for business degrees. So, we are going to be busy (another reason I had decided it was only fair of me to attend). It is now nearly 10am – where is everyone? O says perhaps social work applicants don't like to get up early.

During the day, I speak directly and at length to five would-be applicants. Meanwhile, O has to go and give the presentation. I imagine that many of the potential signed-up attendees go directly to hear her speak as she is providing most of the relevant information that they will need. The people I speak to are both interesting and interested (in social work as a career), but for various reasons. They are all aiming to apply for the course in future: there are three female and two male candidates; three are from overseas (EU nationals or migrants from African countries); and two are of black heritage while three are ethnically white. Their motivations can be briefly described, in no particular order, as follows:

- Someone whose mother was a foster carer and therefore already knows all about social work; being relatively young, this person has no fears about the academic contents of the course either.
- One person is unsure whether they would be accepted onto the course due to personal disability issues but they are reassured to hear (from my colleague when she returns) that one of the keys to becoming a good social worker is being able to make good use of your life experiences.
- Two of the potential candidates are currently working in social care jobs and both say that they enjoy working directly with their clients most of all. One attends today with her husband/partner and is keen to get on and be recognised in a career that offers good opportunities.
- Another person grew up with a father who had substance misuse issues and has therefore acted as a carer; this is also someone who understands all about social work and is enthusiastic to get started on the course.

A note: reflections on these observations

It is interesting to identify some of the reasons that the applicants I met on that particular day had for wanting to take up a career in social work, in addition to those identified in my more recent interviewees' comments. These issues about motivation also connect to published research on this topic (see, for example, Moriarty and Murray, 2007).

Looking back now on my observations, I am somewhat mortified to see how far my perception of myself as an outsider to social work influenced my actions. I describe myself as well established in my academic department, yet I was somewhat reluctant to participate in this very necessary social work educational event at all. (My multidisciplinary department did not only comprise the social work staff group, however.) In retrospect, I hope that in dealing with prospective social work candidates on this and other occasions, I did not let the side down; I would not have disclosed to these prospective students that I was not a social worker (by which I would have intended to help make the day successful), although I do recall saying this quite frequently to my university colleagues at the time.

My good colleague and I enjoyed working together to support the day, which is something that I can personally take from this experience. I think that this narrative does reveal that, to some extent, I had been working with a confused sense of professional identity for many years, despite wanting to be useful to the social work staff and other colleagues (which is another reason why I have included this narrative here) (for more on this, see Chapter 6 on 'Identifying').

Social work: expectations and education

This brings us to an initial consideration of two key questions for social work education and training/continuing professional development (CPD): 'What do social workers need to know?' and, more broadly, 'How is social work education organised and structured?', which I intend to explore initially by using a detailed English example from the early to mid-1990s (for a linked example, see also Chapter 10). As we saw earlier in this chapter, we cannot talk about starting social work with a *tabula rasa* since people bring with them to any career or occupation all kinds of previous understandings/knowledge and experiences, including that gained through earlier careers, occupations or life experiences.

Starting with a perspective based on current, formalised expectations, with which the state concurs, practising social workers in England currently need to conform to the (revised) Professional Capabilities Framework (PCF) that was originally designed in 2012 under the auspices of the College of Social Work, and which contains nine domains[6] (each with detailed level descriptors [see BASW England, 2015]); which now (in 2018) links to the Knowledge and Skills Statements (KSS) for Adults and for Children and Families issued by the two Chief Social Workers. A statement on how these two documents actually link was jointly issued by the British Association of Social Workers (BASW) (which now hosts the PCF on behalf of the social work profession) and the two Chief Social Workers for England. This document states that, 'together, the PCF and KSS provide the foundation for social work education and practice in

England at qualifying and post-qualifying levels and are used to inform recruitment, workforce development, performance appraisal and career progression' (BASW et al, 2018).

Anyone who is unfamiliar with all these written requirements will first be struck by their apparently prescriptive nature; however, on further examination, you will then see how broadly and flexibly they seem to have been conceived and structured. This seems contradictory at first sight. Yet, these official statements also reflect and represent many years of changing policies, curricula and political endeavours; in other words, we can see how they have had to be negotiated by various parties, including the state, social worker organisations and others who may be called 'stakeholders' in these processes. Inevitably perhaps, during these processes, some elements of education and/or practice seem to drop out of the picture, as the following informant discussed with me when considering the change from a previous English framework based on key roles and competences to the current PCF/KSS:

> '*When you look at the PCF ... that was meant to replace the key roles and the competences, um, essentially, it was the same thing being said but in a different way, but with significant omissions in my view. And one of the key omissions was this requirement for social workers to be able to do group work (which is far more cost effective than doing one-to-one casework) had gone completely.... And it's really disappointing ... new social workers now, they are not required to have any idea of group work and that is strictly based, you know, on what we are required to teach them. At the moment, the curriculum is so congested that there is no space to bring in that, you know, and one wonders, well it's not, you don't have to wonder why but, obviously, there's an agenda there.*' (Transnational social worker/educator working in England, interviewed in 2018)

Some recent investigations commissioned by the UK government about the future of social work education (Croisdale-Appleby, 2014; Narey, 2014) have tried to present all this complexity while defining both a level and timescale for social work education: 'A point which emerged time and again from academics, employers, students and practitioners was that we should be educating for a *career*, not training for a job' (Croisdale-Appleby, 2014: 30, emphasis added). This comment seems to reflect what I first noticed when coming into contact with social work (that it is not just a job, but perhaps a calling) and everyone says it is based on values as much as on knowledge or skills. The underlying suggestion from both the aforementioned reports is also that as a career, social work requires a high degree of *academic* success on the part of applicants, and it is felt that, in this way, social work education should lead into a highly skilled and well-regarded profession.

In some countries subject to certain welfare regimes, as we saw in Chapter 3, the state may take on a more or a less important role in these controlling processes (see also Blom et al, 2017; Lyons, 2018), or it can even abolish social work for a time (for example, as in Romania [see Lazăr et al, 2019). For some in the UK, state involvement could also lead to a quite sterile situation. 'There is no comparable system of social-work education in the world which is so nationally uniform, uninspired and tailored so closely to the needs of major state employers'.

So said Chris Jones, (1996: 191), writing of UK social work education in 1996.

As we have seen, when I first came into contact with social work research in 1991, I was aware that the structure and policies surrounding UK social work education were just about to change (from a focus on the official Certificate of Qualification in Social Work (CSS) or Certificate of Qualification in Social Work [CQSW] qualifications into a single, two-year Diploma in Social Work (DipSW), and that this change was reflected in setting up the project I came to work on.

It is certainly true that across Europe, social work education has more recently become firmly situated in higher education institutions, with some key emphasis being placed on academic skills. For example, Branco (2018: 288) speaks of Portuguese social work being influenced by 'a pluralist paradigmatic matrix where critical social work perspectives under the influence of Anglo-Saxon authors coexist with a remaining strong Latin American strand and other orientations, mainly systemic theories and models in social work'. Those with a long history of involvement in social work education have also pointed out that compared with other European countries, social work students in England may spend more time in work-based practice ('placements'), and so education for practice has itself become much more regulated there (see Lyons, 2018). According to Lyons, this could also be an explanation for the frequent separation of education and training in some contexts.

In terms of professional scope, we have already noted in Chapter 3 that in countries such as Switzerland (according to one of my informants), a generic qualification could include social work, social pedagogy and youth and community work, and this would then allow graduates to work in a variety of social settings. A Danish social work educator also told me that due to their slightly different role in social practice, those trained in social pedagogy (see also Cameron, 2004) have less training in some aspects of law that are required for social workers in Denmark:

> '[Social workers] *make decisions about* [family] *placements and things like that. So, bachelors in social work in Denmark have a lot of training in doing casework, a lot of training in law, you know, and I don't think pedagogues have that … many courses in law and legislation around child welfare and employment and things like that, that's specific for social work.'* (Danish social work educator, interviewed in 2018)

Casting my mind back to 1991 in the UK, when policies and the political climate were (ostensibly) very different from today, there were nevertheless similar questions being asked, not to say priorities being set, concerning what was considered appropriate *content* for social work education (and training). The *organisation and structure* of social work education were also undergoing changes at that time aimed at 'improving' the quality and quantity of social workers, and also refining the structure of how education, training and continuing professional development (CPD) were delivered. In the early 1990s, in addition to the move into the DipSW qualification, key policy discourses in social work practice and education had begun to reflect an underlying and quite fundamental split between work with children and families and with adults. Following the UK Children Act 1989, attempts were being made to, for example, set work with children and families on a path towards greater emphasis on measurable outcomes concerning effectiveness (see, for example, Parker, 1991; Ward, 1995); meanwhile, adult social work was clearly being focused around the notion of Community Care. These processes were reflected in various ways in the formal plans for social work and social care education and training. As a very experienced social worker commented to me in England in 2018:

> 'one of the biggest splits is that it's gone from being a generic profession to being politically … determined by two separate government departments, and adults and children's social work, there's been a big divide created between them … so I think in that sense, you know, that's sort of, I think for me, the biggest change in the time that I've been a social worker, but, on the other

hand, that division has also allowed adults and children's work to specialise more, to strengthen and consolidate more, around what its standards are, what it's doing.'

This kind of developing specialisation was also commented on by some of my European interviewees in 2018, for example:

'the bureaucratisation of practice is one thing that happened after my qualification [in 1998]. *Also, the more predefined methodologies to work were in certain fields like, for instance, child protection. Child protection was already a big field of social work intervention* [in Portugal], *but it was after my qualification that it became a field of work much more predefined, with very strict steps to follow.'*

While a consideration of 'adults' social work thus only represents part of the social work story, I feel that by examining my own involvement with social work educational policy and Community Care in the 1990s in some detail, the following example illustrates the complicated nature of constructing a new, revised social work qualification (the DipSW) that would try to suit everyone: the professional regulator (the Central Council for Education and Training in Social Work [CCETSW] at that time), employers, educational institutions/staff, students, the wider workforce, service users, and carers. I will follow up this example in Chapter 10 by exploring how training underpinning the new Community Care policies was envisaged, using another auto-ethnographic example from the same time period in the 1990s and including a brief examination of my participation in events convened to disseminate information and explore the changing policy landscape.

A case example: reflections on Community Care and changing social work education programmes

I remember Community Care having a very influential part to play in relation to social work education and wider workforce training (as well as in social work policy and practice more widely) from the early 1990s onwards. Language around Community Care was such that many people commented to me at the time (at workshops, conferences and so on) that, in one sense, 'everyone knows' what it means and yet 'nobody does'. I also heard people say that it was 'impossible to disagree' with the concept of Community Care precisely because of its component parts: who could disagree with the ideas of 'community' or of 'care'? Key underpinning themes were that Community Care for vulnerable adults was inherently multi- (or inter-)professional, requiring a considerable amount of collaboration between different agencies involved in providing care. There was also much emphasis on the empowerment of users of services and those involved as (informal) carers – developing what was termed formally as a 'needs-led' approach (see, for example, Beresford, 1994). I also remember that some social workers and employers that I encountered were unsure at the time about whether the direction that these policies were taking was the right one, particularly in achieving a balance between health and social care (for a more medicalised perspective on Community Care, see, for example, Groves, 1993). I certainly encountered some social workers who were reluctant to embrace what we would now label as 'neoliberal' developments, which included a split between the purchasing and providing of services and of relevant training; this all reflected the concept of a mixed economy of care, with all of its implications for workforce skills and knowledge.

From the research work that I was involved in since 1991, I had understood that the Griffiths Report (1989) (leading to the NHS and Community Care Act 1990) had prompted CCETSW to set up a five-year Community Care Programme (ending in the financial year 1994/95), in which money was earmarked to support the identification of knowledge and skills for Community Care, as well as for the promotion of appropriate education and training. This included more emphasis on the inclusion of users of services (see, for example, Beresford, 1994; London Community Care Action Group, 1994; Lindow, and Morris, 1995). The 1990 Act was not implemented until 1993, partly, I imagine, in order to allow time for these complex administrative, policy, practice and educational changes to be made.[7]

Following on from my initial involvement in the second part of the CCETSW-King's College (C-K) project,[8] I was asked to do a review, based on a content analysis of documents emanating from different institutions running social work education programmes, concerning the proposed DipSW curricula that they had submitted for validation (approval) to the official regulator, CCETSW London and South-East England Region. (This project is reported on in more depth by its director [as Stage 3 of the C-K project] in Whittington, 1998.)

While working with King's College and then during project work at CCETSW London and South-East England region itself, I subsequently became involved in a wider survey of purchasers and providers of Community Care training as part of the organisation's five-year Community Care programme (I discuss my involvement in this survey further in Chapter 10 of this volume, 'Organising').

In Stage 3 of the C–K project, Whittington (1998: ch 9) reports that by 1991, the original 22 CQSW and four CSS programmes examined in the first two parts of the C–K project were being reshaped into 19 (university- or college-based) DipSW programmes within the CCETSW London and South-East England region. All these programmes were expected to be partnerships between educational institutions and employers (Whittington refers to these as 'agencies') (see also CCETSW, 1991). The programmes, offered at universities and colleges registered with CCETSW, included both separate, two-year (non-graduate and postgraduate) diploma programmes and degrees that included the diploma.[9] I was asked to examine 'the formally-declared intentions of programme designers' (Whittington, 1998: 277) and to rely in the analysis on their documentation alone. Whittington (1998: 277) reports that I described these submissions as 'kinds of "scripts" that programmes had developed in order to present the philosophy of the course, its structure and curriculum and, in particular, assessment. As scripts they would not be permanently fixed but subject to review and development'.

I would add here that much of my thinking about how to do an analysis of this material would have come from my attempts to understand processes with which I was not necessarily familiar. This anthropological approach allowed me to treat the material as an outsider would, and thus interrogate and question certain aspects of the proposed DipSW programmes (but resources did not permit interviewing any respondents). I could see, for example, that participants sometimes struggled to cover all aspects of the organisational and inter-professional areas in their documentation (results that we subdivided into specific topics to be taught and assessed, having been identified in our project as being relevant to Community Care).[10] As Whittington (1998: 277) also says, some former CQSW teachers also thought that 'the change to the DipSW introduced an overly-regulated qualification'. Meanwhile, I focused on language use in the documents under review; one thing that I remember noting was that social work programme staff, and perhaps our own project team, seemed to me to have moved from using the term 'competence' in a common-sense way (as in simply 'being competent') into describing 'competences' as 'things' to be applied. I recall our project team having many happy arguments about my interpretation of this as a 'change of language use'! In any event, I think using the term 'scripts' gave us all a sense of what social work educators were grappling with on the ground within these submitted materials.

At that time, I had not experienced working in a university-based DipSW programme myself (which would come later on), so I was intrigued to discover what was required as part of the proposed social work curricula: this included specific courses (or modules) such as Areas of Particular Practice (APPs). These were typically offered to students in fields such as children and families work, probation, adult services and/or Community Care, reflecting contemporary areas of social work specialism; these were intended to provide students with both knowledge and in-depth practice experience in the chosen areas. These APPs mirrored the policy changes towards a clear split between work with adults and with children, which has become an even deeper division within social work policy and practice over recent years. Whittington (1998: 291) reported that ten out of the 19 DipSW programmes whose materials I was examining offered an APP in Community Care. Furthermore, in addition to relevant generic skills, some of the nine skills and knowledge areas that we had identified as of particular relevance to Community Care (including areas such as the 'costing of care plans' or 'community care assessments') were intended to be assessed only for students taking the Community Care APP rather than for all social work students. (This could arguably have implications for their future job roles after qualification.)

In terms of key changes in proposed curriculum content between the earlier CQSW and CSS programmes and the planned DipSW programmes, Whittington provides further details by comparing results from Stage 1 and Stage 3 of the C-K project in his conclusions (Whittington, 1998: ch 10). These conclusions clearly suggest that, overall, areas of learning for *organisational and inter-professional competence* were more evident in the DipSW than in the former social work qualifications; for example, teaching students about working in teams, using computerised systems, using (social) networks and inter-professional collaboration, as well as greater commitment to empowering service users and carers, had all become more visible within the DipSW curricula. However, specific assessment of students in some of these areas of the curriculum was not always evident (Whittington, 1998: ch 10).

Chapter 4 summary

This chapter has focused on issues relating to social work education and training in the UK and, comparatively, in a few other countries. I have identified some initial themes relevant to taking an anthropological perspective, specifically:

- 'Becoming': motivation – with examples from recent interviews with informants and an auto-ethnographic example.
- What do social workers need to know? A question to which a brief introductory discussion of current trends was provided.
- The structure and content of education and training was introduced using a 1990s' policy example relating to Community Care in which I participated directly (see also Chapter 10).

This chapter has set the scene for further discussions in later chapters, and links to Chapter 5 ('Growing') on experiencing social work education, from student and educator perspectives.

Notes

[1]   Lyons (2018: 5) speaks of those involved in networks of professional education across Europe taking 'a pragmatic approach to the question "what constitutes social work?" and [they] coined the term "social professions" as a more inclusive description of the field'.

[2]   Pawlas-Czyz et al (2017) discuss the relationship of social workers and 'family assistants' in Poland.

[3]   See Hussein (2014).

[4]   Example findings from Moriarty and Murray's (2007) study, using the Universities and Colleges Admissions Service (UCAS) data, showed that: around half of those accepted onto the (current) three-year social work degree in the UK were aged over 25; men were 'less likely to apply' than women (Moriarty and Murray, 2007: 722); and 'the proportion of Black people accepted for social work is among the highest for any subject' (Moriarty and Murray, 2007: 723).

[5]   As ever, I am presenting myself here as the 'outsider'.

[6]   These domains cover: (1) professionalism; (2) values and ethics; (3) diversity and equality; (4) rights, justice and economic well-being; (5) knowledge; (6) critical reflection and analysis; (7) skills and interventions; (8) contexts and organisations; and (9) professional leadership.

[7]   As Griffiths himself (in Groves, 1993: xii) cautiously wrote: 'authorities will have had three years to think through the final implementation [of the 1990 Act]. This staged process ... has gone reasonably well, but the brave new world will reveal itself only gradually'.

[8]   Parts 1 and 2 of this project covered CCETSW's London and South-East England region and focused respectively on: (1) a review of organisational and inter-professional content in the curricula of the 22 regional CQSW and four CSS programmes (in 1990); and (2) a postal survey of social workers (including probation officers taking the same programme[s] in all service sectors, qualifying in 1990 [the final year before the DipSW was

introduced]). For more details, see Whittington (1998) and Whittington and Bell (1992, 2001).

9   My notes from the time also show that by 1992, CCETSW London and South-East England region had formally approved 14 of these DipSW programmes, 18 practice learning agencies and 16 practice teacher programmes.

10 Whittington (1998: 279 ff) groups the results about proposed curriculum content and student assessment from Stage 3 of the C–K project into the following topic areas: Knowledge of the organisation; Skills in working with others in organisations; Values and expectations; Knowledge of other organisations and professions; Skills in working with other organisations and professions; and Community Care.

Growing: experiencing social work education and socialisation

In Chapter 4, we first examined some social workers' motivations for embarking on a social work career; then, via an example from 1990s' England, we also looked at how social work education is 'constructed' from the point of view of some of those controlling or implementing educational policy in the social work field. We noted the growing influences on social work in the 1990s of health policy, of inter-professional and multi-agency approaches, and of attempts to extend the influence of users of services and carers, in tandem with evolving political policies. Underpinning all of this discussion are the continuing issues of power and control (who decides what and how people learn and practise).

In this chapter, I want to return to the experiences of those becoming socialised into social work, and of the educators who participate in this socialising. In my recent interviews with social workers across Europe, I found that about half of them (like me) had had some involvement with social work education or training, in addition to engaging in social work practice, and that for experienced workers, this focus on education and/or training was especially significant during the latter part of their careers.

As well as teaching social work students in English higher education for several years, I also had some involvement with exploring the experiences of those who were students, fellow educators and social work practitioners during various research projects. Therefore, this chapter will draw upon some of this material, as well as on my more recent key informant interviews.

Here is a final-year undergraduate social work student in England connecting up the nature of their course and their experiences of learning with their overall understanding of social work:

> '*I think there's becoming more and more of an emphasis on self-directed learning and, I mean, self-directed learning is grand, but the nature of social work is about human interaction and I have concerns about shifting even more to e-learning and stuff like that, where I think we need face to face, and that's where you hear of*

practice issues, dynamics, how people deal with stuff and you can't really learn that via a computer.'[1]

In the following extract, the same student responds to a question about the importance of organisational issues for effective learning:

Focus group facilitator: *'How important is it for students to receive guidance about dealing with organisational issues, such as timetables, timekeeping, what sort of time management and dealing with colleagues and stuff like that, within your tutor groups? Organisational stuff, how important is it?'*

Student: *'I think we probably spent a lot of our first year doing that because a lot of people were returning to study or being mature students, so you needed to understand how the university works and, well, the basics.'*

A social work educator speaking during the same project said:

'We talk about, you know, being a social work student within an organisation and how they function. So, you're looking at their professional, personal-professional development within the organisation, as well as the direct work [that is, with clients/service users[2]], *and that's all material I would expect to be discussed.'*

Another tutor (a qualified social worker) interviewed for this project said:

'I think perhaps the tutor group might be even more important for MA students, given that they start placement on day three of their experience on the programme, so they're having to get their heads around being at a brand new university potentially, studying at master's level, finding their way in a new environment and starting at a first assessed practice learning placement, that's a lot for anybody to deal with at one time, and I think that the tutorial [group] *and the tutor provides some support around managing all of that.'*

These comments reflect the fact that social work students and their educators include work within the university or college, where social work education is taught, as well as the outside settings in which direct social work with clients/service users is practised, as organisational issues. As we found when conducting our tutor groups research project, the tutor group setting itself (though convened at the university/college) thus occupies a marginal or liminal space that is somehow between the academic world and the practice placement, which some students already thought was the 'real world' (see Jones, 2015; see also Chapter 11, this volume, 'Symbolising').

To further explain what I mean, in the following extract, a first-year postgraduate student taking a qualifying-level social work programme, who had recently started on the job in a student placement, speaks about the significance of this ambiguous tutor group space:

> 'I think needing to have space to do that is definitely important, especially regarding [the work] placement because it's, it's outside of here, it's kind of ... it's sort of separate from the university and we need to sort of link in with our tutors and make sure that if there's any issue with the placement, that the universities can get involved and kind of intervene and see if there's any way of resolving that. Because I know that people do have issues with placements or with practice assessors and the sooner you ... get that resolved, the better; so, I would say that's incredibly important to be able to discuss like placement issues and have space to do that. And it's good to do that in the group as well because, obviously, other people sometimes have the same experience and kind of ... the group kind of chips in on how best to ... address something, you know; have you tried this, have you tried that?'

As another social work educator/tutor said when speaking about the overall purpose of the tutor groups within the social work programmes: "there is an academic component, there's a practice component, but there's another pastoral component which they don't get anywhere else".

A key area of socialisation into social work involves dealing with emotions and relationships, as previously mentioned (see also Chapter 7, this volume). Here are two undergraduate social work students speaking to each other (for the same project) about how their group support enables them to cope with these emotional aspects of the work:

Student 1:   'There's a difference between being autonomous and being isolated, and without the tutor groups you become isolated.'

Student 2:   'And especially for social work, because it is so emotionally demanding and it is such a big day going out on *placement. I think just that issue of looking after yourself and having somebody there who's able to give you advice on that. How to stay sane and how to deal with difficult situations.'*

These comments by students and tutors begin to reflect some of the initial issues involved in becoming socialised as a social work professional during social work education; therefore, we will next consider the process of socialisation itself in more detail.

Experiencing socialisation as an accomplishment

In anthropological terms, continuing socialisation assumes a significant focus for any occupation or profession (for an American view of socialisation into social work, see Miller, 2010). I am taking the view here that growing as a social worker is about accomplishing something, about constructing a knowledgeable identity and expertise, all based on acknowledging what are considered to be appropriate values. As well as place, space and organisation, this also takes a considerable amount of time (see later). In addition to the more formal aspects of learning that we are discussing in this chapter, socialisation therefore involves aspects that I would describe as: deciding on (or at least acknowledging) a motivation towards 'doing what social workers do' and what they believe in; making continuing use of practical experiences with users/recipients of services in order to build a career and an identity; collaborating with other professionals (including other social workers); and taking up voluntary or paid employment with an appropriate agency (or, on occasions, as an independent professional). Meanwhile, all of this is taking place within changing professional and policy contexts (see, for example, my discussion with co-authors, linking time, experience and analytical reflection, with examples from Norway, Denmark and England, in Bell et al, 2017).

How are we to conceptualise these processes of accomplishment? When social work students are in training, as I indicated earlier, they are most often participating within a cohort of fellow students, and while each must learn how to practise social work as an individual, collaborative efforts to grow into their profession must surely be significant. In some, but not all, social work educational programmes, this takes place within formalised tutor group settings, such as those that I and my colleagues have researched. There may be differences in how students and their educators view these processes. A key finding from our tutor groups project was that while both 'staff and students recognise the support and monitoring functions of tutor groups … students emphasise the supportive function whilst staff highlight the monitoring of student progression and development, and fitness for practice' (Bell and Villadsen, 2010: 5).

Several of my recent social worker informants did comment on the importance of time in allowing people to grow into their 'social work self'. Many of these informants were doubtful about trying to achieve this within restricted time frames; for example, where students can now become qualified practitioners through a shorter course than was envisaged when setting up (across Europe) the current three-year social work degree. One social work educator said:

> '[As a social worker,] *you are a person who's developing a certain body of knowledge, obviously, but also a certain way of being that includes your values, your interpersonal skills and communication skills, and I do think that growing into that kind of identity and way of being takes more than two years.'* (Transnational social worker/educator interviewed in 2018)

Another English social worker who was in favour of a longer lead-in to social work education, for example, via an apprenticeship, said that "*Academia doesn't necessarily mean social work skills and although people are very good conceptually, they still have to make that transformation, and in an accelerated programme, that's very hard*" (social worker/educator interviewed in 2018).

Elsewhere in Europe, I found that social work students were also receiving part of their education through 'doing practice', and that in this, they were getting support from educators within the university and also from outside practitioners. The following social work educator from Romania, whom I interviewed in 2018, said:

> '*The first year* [students] *are not supposed to do practice, but after that first semester, in every semester, they have placements. They have in one semester, each week, one day of practice. So, it's spread throughout the semester, which leads to about 14 days of practice, and this is for six hours a day each week … and supplementary to this, we have introduced in* [our university] *(in other centres, it's not like this) a lab, which we call "coaching and mentoring", and we invited … for instance, in* [our university] *we have more than 20 associated social workers actually from, with practice experience, a lot of practice experience, who discuss every week with the students about their practice experience and reflect on what happened and*

something like that, which is complementary to this placement,
which is in the field, but we have this at the university. So, they
have eight hours, I would say, a week for related, practice related.'

As an example from a non-Western society that connects with the idea of group learning through experience, the anthropologist Barth (1975) writes in his book about ritual and knowledge in a small society (of 183 people) situated in New Guinea (the Baktaman). He describes how boys are initiated via age-based cohorts into knowledge relevant to their society. Barth argues that in this context, 'culture' comprises 'an ongoing system of communication [that] contains a corpus of replicated messages' (Barth, 1975: 15). I suggest that this concept of 'replicated messages' is useful for us to consider as being (at least in part) what constitutes social work learning and (more formal) education within these kinds of collaborative endeavours.[3] The process of passing on these messages to new recruits and professionals (at all stages of their careers) thus implies learning what is expected of you not only by (future or existing) employers, but also by professional colleagues and society at large.[4]

Social workers, especially in Western societies, are specialists who are somehow motivated to choose their profession as individuals, and who are expected to critically reflect on their practice; this form of reflective individualism can also be seen as a wider feature of Westernised societies. However, as noted earlier, for social workers, significance is placed on the 'doing' of certain actions, especially during their education and training. As another comparison, the anthropologist Byron Good (1994), writing about the profession of medicine, describes how trainee doctors' experiences of the body are constructed, especially by 'doing', during their medical education. He also usefully links this idea to what he considers to be our civilisation's 'deep commitment' to 'biological individualism', and suggests that medicine is 'deeply implicated' in our 'image of what constitutes suffering', as well as the means of redemption from it (Good, 1994: 86). We can surely connect social workers, as representatives of another caring profession, to these underlying arguments, even though (as we have already seen in earlier chapters) one of the heavily contested fault lines within these professions, and in terms of policy and structure in any Western society, is that between what constitutes the realm of 'health/medicine' and what is perceived as 'social'.

Barth's book describes Baktaman efforts to control for themselves how different levels of knowledge can be passed on through various grades of initiation in their small society, as well as what is passed on.

Good discusses various aspects of (more formalised) medical curricula in Western societies, alongside his discussions about knowledge of healing in various other societies. I suggest that the processes being described in both these examples provide a useful model for what is happening during social work education, especially in terms of connecting with what social workers term professional 'practice'. Crucially, both Good and Barth also discuss symbolic elements of meaning that will be useful in my later discussions (see particularly Chapter 11, this volume).

Thinking about learning: what, how and why?

What do social workers themselves think they should learn and what are the different possibilities in terms of theoretical approaches to social work as a discipline? We have already seen in previous chapters what the state, especially in England, thinks social workers formally need to know, and this reflects what the official views of their roles are. However, that is not necessarily the whole story. I also gave an example in Chapter 2 of how a meta-theoretical view of differing approaches to social work helped me to appreciate that not all social workers think or practise in the same way.

The following experienced social worker, now working in English social work education, suggested to me in her recent interview (in 2018) how curriculum content and overall policies towards social work are linked:

> 'If you think what a social worker needs to know is the law and the policy of the agency and how to talk to people, then what you do to educate is a very different thing than if you think social work is part of the International, you know, Federation of Social Work definition, about including social justice etc., then your education is different isn't it?... [In the first case,] you'd do a little bit of sociology, but you won't have an in-depth understanding of the social sciences.'

Another recently interviewed informant, who qualified in England in the 1980s, signed up at that time for a four-year degree, the final part of which comprised two years of training in social work. This, she felt, gave her an excellent introduction to the field:

> 'in those first two years [of the social sciences degree], we literally did every discipline in the social sciences. We did a module

in each, we did about eight modules across the two years and I feel that that really gave me a good grounding to understand what social issues were from all different perspectives. And then on that course, you could opt to do a pathway, one of which was social work for two years, where you then trained in the skills that you needed and you did theory of social work and skills.... So, I think, for me, that was a unique time and was a very, very good way of training to be a social worker, which I don't think that people have to any degree now.'

There are clearly practice-based and philosophical differences in the ways in which social workers can operate or think about their profession in terms of theory and practice (and, indeed, whether a distinction can or should be made between them). As mentioned earlier and in the Chapters 1 and 2, there had already been attempts, which I found useful, to map the various underlying schools of thought that can be explored and absorbed by students of social work and subsequently used in social work practice(s); yet, these cannot be seen as static or unchanging (see Whittington and Holland, 1985; Holland, 1999). Arguably, as the previous informant suggests, a broad understanding of the social sciences would be a useful grounding for someone starting to learn about social work. For nearly all of the social workers I talked to, in addition to their theoretical learning, it is the way in which underpinning philosophies and epistemologies can be made to link to more specific theories and to social work practice that seems key to their understanding of their profession.

I came to understand that one key underpinning series of frameworks for much current social work practice and theory revolves around the ideas of *systems* and *systemic practice*.[5] Healy (2014: 122), for example, describes how earlier social work theory drew from general systems theory (GST) and then from ecological models, a metaphor that social workers could use (for example, in their work with families) 'to focus on transactions within and across systems and to seek sustainable, not only short-term, change'. Discussing the work by Gitterman and Germain (2008 [1996]), Healy (2014: 121–35) assesses how their 'life model of social work practice' and other systems approaches have both advantages and limitations. On the one hand, a focus on structure and function has the advantage of enabling social workers to understand and respond to people in their environment, and at the different levels of individual, group and community. On the other hand, there are always questions about how to clearly define the boundaries of any system. Does taking a systemic approach also discourage social workers from looking back into the causes of behaviour or thinking? Is a structural/functional focus inconsistent with social work values (for example, in relation to systemic issues of power or injustice)?

Moving on to other theoretical and practice-based influences, one influential way of thinking about what has been termed 'clinical' social work can involve taking a *psychoanalytically informed focus*, providing a link between social work and psychoanalytic theory. According to some commentators, this clinical (psychoanalytical) approach has maintained its current influence in social work and social work education, and is recently experiencing a resurgence of interest (see, for example, Cooper, 2015). Cooper points out that promoters of this approach, such as the Tavistock Centre in London, have had a long-standing role in social work education (within the National Health Service [NHS] in the UK), as well as enabling the production of relevant publications (such as the *Journal of Social Work Practice*) (Cooper, personal communication; see also Cooper, 2015). Relationship-based practice and 'practice-near' research and observation are particularly significant to this approach (see, for example, Bryan et al, 2016; Hingley-Jones et al, 2017). As Bryan, Hingley-Jones and Ruch (2016: 229) suggest: 'In our view, relationship underpins social work practice in all its forms. We believe that social worker–service user relationships are strengthened by a deeper understanding of the psychodynamics and emotions of those relationships, set within the systems and organisational contexts in which these interactions take place'.

Contemporary use of these kinds of concepts within relationship-based practice does not rule out links to other approaches, such as systemic work, as Hyare (2015: 104) suggests:

> relationship-based practice thus requires attention to individual relationships beyond that between the practitioner and the service user; to the context of the vulnerable people we work with; and also importantly to the organisational context that social workers work within, and relationship between both individuals (service users and practitioners) and organisations to the macro socio-economic-political context that all parties operate within. Psychoanalytic concepts in combination with attachment theory and systems theory afford an opportunity to consider all of these factors when undertaking assessment and interventions.

Nevertheless, where their main focus has been on internal individual development, psychoanalytic approaches have been criticised by some who have argued that they have moved social work away from what they see as its original community-based mission, especially in certain geographical settings such as the US (see, for example, Specht and Courtney, 1994).

Some social workers have called for radical approaches to social work based on materialist premises, informed by Marxist theory, and community-based social movements, which can result in resistance to neoliberal developments in particular (see, for example, Ferguson and Lavalette, 2004; Ferguson, 2008). However, writing in 1998, Langan (1998: 207) suggested that 'The moment of radical social work has now passed [although] many of its defining values [of community, quality, feminism, anti-racism and so on] have entered the mainstream of social work practice'. More recent commentators such as Carey and Foster (2011) have suggested that such radical approaches can still be teased out in practice, for example, through examining small-scale, day-to-day acts of resistance, perceived as 'positive deviance' (DSW – deviant social work) by social workers. However, these authors (Carey and Foster (2011: 578) suggest that these attitudes and practices are distinct from, albeit linked to, radical social work, being 'predominately non-collective and individual ... not necessarily explicitly tied to a critical or "emancipatory" ideological agenda and, yet, ironically ... for the most part a response to the control related processes that radical social workers identified as a priority'.

This brief discussion around various schools of thought is meant to illustrate a few examples of social work's underpinning philosophies and practices, as well as to suggest how some social work rationales, especially the psychoanalytic/psychodynamic and the radical, have waxed and waned over time. The origins of radical social work are said to lie in the 1970s and 1980s, with psychoanalytic themes going even further back in time; yet, these approaches appear to have reinvented themselves and to have been reclaimed by their adherents more recently. A key question for any observer who understands that social workers may be influenced by differing theoretical positions is, then: how exactly do these get transmitted to students and what might a social work educator's priorities be when teaching social work students? (For further discussion about 'knowing and evidencing' in practice, see also Chapter 9.)

Looking in more detail at what social workers are expected to learn and practise, you will remember that in Chapter 4, we identified the current requirements of the Professional Capabilities Framework (PCF) and Knowledge and Skills Statements (KSS) for social workers in England. Although these practice requirements appear fairly generalised, at the level of social work education, they imply the need for greater scrutiny. However, this raises further issues about how such an agenda can be realistically achieved in future, as the following recently interviewed social worker/educator suggests:

Informant: '*I think for social work education, there's going to be more scrutiny. So, I think the inspectors will come and observe teaching. I think they will look at the curriculum and so I think there will be greater scrutiny. For the profession, it's going to be much tighter regulation, so even when you qualify as a social worker, you will have to be accredited* [for example, for working in child protection], *so you will have to do multiple choice questionnaires* [MCQs], *have your practice observed and if you don't meet the standard, you get one more go to do it and you're out....*

One of the service managers talked to me because he did it as a trial run and he said some of the questions were completely ridiculous on the [accreditation] *MCQ because in social work, there often isn't a right or a wrong answer. The only place there is a right or wrong answer is with the law. So, give me this bit of the law, section 2, does it say this, that and that? But if you say "Should this older person have meals on wheels?", or "Should that older person have ...?"'*

Interviewer: '*So, it's more of a judgement, professional judgement?*'

Informant: '*Yes it is, so I don't know how they're going to ...*' (Social worker/educator speaking in England in 2018)

Once social workers formally qualify, they are expected to keep up to date with their own professional development on a regular basis when they are employed. I identified many examples in my recent interviews of social workers training and retraining, sometimes in different specialisms, either while working with the same employer or when moving jobs. Someone who was interviewed as part of my earlier research projects into professional education and training (see, for example, Bell, 2007a) provided some useful insights into what this can mean for these staff and their employers:

'*I think that we still have a long way to go in terms of really, really understanding the way in which the impact that training and development can actually have on people's capacity to do*

71

the job I, I think we're still in the very early stages of actually understanding that, and understanding what it is that really enables people to work at their full potential, because training and development has to be understood in a wider context, which is what the organisation is itself, how the organisation in itself enables people to do their job....

Part of the learning is doing the job, so I think we still have to do a lot more work around the evaluation process, and really helping people themselves to try and evaluate, you know, "How has that really made a difference?", "How has my work actually changed?", so I suppose it's something about ... what still needs to happen is to encourage people to be able to reflect on their own work and their own skills and their own effectiveness, and not be afraid of that.' (Social work training manager/educator working in a local authority, interviewed in 2006)

These views were echoed by a social worker/educator working in Europe who I interviewed recently, and who expressed optimism about the future, provided that social workers could learn to balance their creativity with accountability:

'If we let our practice be reduced to some small standardised steps, we don't need a scientific profession, a scientific-based profession any more. So, for me, that's a real danger. So, we have to find ways to respond to that and I think one way is to train students to be more proactive, to have more initiative, but also to be very technically competent and not be afraid of being accountable and having to show results. I think we have to learn how to dialogue with this kind of neoliberal approach and vocabulary, working on the deconstruction of that kind of vocabulary.' (Social worker/social work educator from Portugal, interviewed in 2018)

Once again, this social worker suggests how *language* (particularly relating to neoliberalism) needs to be challenged and used in debate, especially during social work education, in order to allow social workers to learn to work within changing policy contexts.

A social worker who was working in English higher education when I interviewed him a few years ago (as part of projects that I was conducting about social workers' understandings of knowledge and evidence [see Bell, 2008]) usefully suggested that the social work educator's role was, in his view, a very complex one:

'*Some people who are educators and trainers, who are good practitioners, but because of the limitation of their theoretical sophistication ... they interact with the students in a way which is often quite crude. And, I don't think it's pragmatic, because pragmatic is good. It's not sufficiently sophisticated and pragmatic....*

But at the other extreme, there are some people who teach social policy for social workers at a level of abstraction without really showing how then particular problems do get constructed and how you can intervene in that; so you've got the intellectual shallowness, or the theoretical distance, too much distance, and what we grow towards in social work is trying to integrate the two.'

Reflecting on these examples and my conversations with these social workers and others, I can see that the often-stated attempt to 'link theory and practice'[6] in social work education is much more complicated than I had originally thought, especially when I first began to teach social workers about research. It took me many years to make research relevant to social workers, and particularly to address difficult areas such as their (lack of) use and appreciation of quantitative research methods (see Bell and Clancy, 2013; Bell, 2017: ch 6).

I also began to gradually understand that my own focus on doing and appreciating research tended to cut out the personal and emotional aspects that social workers were all striving to accomplish in their own professional development. Eventually, I realised that my motivation towards my own professions of research and (previously) information work was perhaps a way of helping people that was devoid of (what was, for me) too much emotional content. The example in Box 5.1 may help to illustrate what I mean.

Box 5.1: The scream: a disturbing event, or how I did not know what to do

When visiting a local authority social services office to speak to staff about our research project in the early 1990s, we were aware on leaving of someone screaming in an anguished way in the main entrance hall, where we had entered the building. While apologising to us, our contact calmly showed us out by a different exit. This event left me stunned and disturbed, and I have remembered it ever since. I did not want to discuss the event with my colleagues on the CCETSW-King's College (C-K) project, one of whom had accompanied me. Reflecting on what happened that day makes me aware that I felt helpless in that situation and did not have any idea of what I might do to help this person. In fact, I just wanted to get away.

Many years later, I read Malcolm Payne's (2006: 53–5) account (which he calls the story of 'The screaming woman') in which, as a newly qualified social worker, he used his own experience and skills (including a basic knowledge of hypnosis) to actually deal with a situation not unlike this one. He suggests that this kind of experience is common to many social workers and that when intervening in the personal aspects of people's lives in the public interest, this implies several key aspects of personal interaction with clients/service users, which we can summarise as:

• human communication within a relationship;
• recognising that 'social work is a process';
• realising that 'specific values lie beneath all social work activities';
• the need to reconstruct knowledge based on both personal experience and academic knowledge; and
• use of self.

For a non-social worker, Payne's example brings out both the complexity and the underlying humanity involved in actually doing social work. There is a clear mixing of theoretical, personal and skilful elements here. As we saw in earlier chapters, it also implies that the social worker has to be motivated to do something to address such personal distress; however, I would also argue, from my own experience recounted earlier, that not everyone may be emotionally capable of taking this kind of action, even with appropriate training. This brings us to Chapter 6, 'Identifying'.

Chapter 5 summary

In this chapter, I have explored the views of some social workers and social work students about socialisation into their profession and provided some background about this concept from an anthropological perspective. I have begun to explore what social workers think they should learn and have set this against epistemological background material describing some key frameworks for social work theory and practice. Using an experience relating to personal interaction and the use of self, this chapter leads into a discussion of identity in Chapter 6.

Notes

[1] This quote is taken from interview, focus group and ethnographic material gathered in 2008/09 as part of a research project into tutor groups at one English university. These groups, which were facilitated by an experienced social worker, offered collective support to small groups of university-based social work students within the larger, annual student cohorts (see Bell and Villadsen, 2010, 2011; Bell, 2017). I acknowledge my colleague and collaborator Dr Aase Villadsen, who facilitated the student focus groups for this project.

[2] Direct work involves relationships and the emotions that go with them, and this is always and everywhere perceived as a key area for social workers. I will also address this separately in Chapter 7.

[3] There are also parallels here with 'replicated messages' emerging and being passed on from the educational policy developments that I describe in the 'Community Care' case examples (in Chapters 4 and 10).

[4] I am aware of many difficulties in comparing 'Westernised' with other kinds of societies; others have also written about the relevance of drawing on indigenous knowledge in social work (a profession with considerable potential for Eurocentrism, despite its international focus [see, for example, Dumbrill and Green, 2008]). I attempt to use Barth's anthropological concept of 'a corpus of replicated messages' (albeit in a more limited way) in order to try and draw together similar socialisation processes in different societies.

[5] These ideas remain influential in the UK (see, for example, Department for Education, 2017).

[6] See the interesting discussion in Beresford, Adshead and Croft (2007: ch 11) about social work theory and practice (in this case, in the context of palliative care social work) and the assertion that there has been 'very limited involvement from service users in the development of social work theory' (Beresford et al, 2007: 174). According to these authors, service users have been developing their own theories and discourses.

6

Identifying

In this chapter, I come to a key issue for both social workers and those who work alongside them: identity. I have already suggested that I see identity or identities as something that social workers (and those in related occupations, such as social pedagogues) construct with others, especially as they become socialised into their profession. In earlier chapters, we saw that both Jenkins (2014) and Chandler (2017) characterise identity as something that can be both collective and individual. As the following social work interviewee said to me, there are issues with defining the collective form of social work identity, which will have implications for individual practitioners:

> '*We have really struggled with this idea of our professional identity and we have both striven for, but had it imposed upon us, what that identity is; and I think largely due to nervousness about the role, I think you start to mention child protection and people, you know, the government etc, feel very anxious and their anxiety, this is my take on it, is therefore, they feel it's important to standardise, have very clear-cut expectations.*' (English social worker/educator speaking in 2018)

As we saw in Chapter 5, this standardisation can involve increasing controls over social work education as well as practice, though some have suggested that, where possible, social workers need to learn how to balance accountability with creativity. There have been recent attempts to put in place specific forms of post-qualification accreditation (for example, for social workers working in child protection in England), though the outcome of that particular attempt is still uncertain at the time of writing.

Some informants also said to me that they thought the social work role was becoming narrower, or distributed to other professions or occupations:

> '*The social work role is being distributed to other groups. So, police officers take on more of the work of social workers, school teachers take on more of the role, nurses take on more of the role of social workers, charities with people not qualified in social work but who*

might do some of the tasks and roles that people used to take, and social work is being reduced to a very narrow activity, which is concerned with safeguarding and corporate parenting.'

Some of my earlier research with a colleague explored issues relating to social work students' attitudes towards other professionals and the potential impact on development of their professional identities (see Bell and Allain, 2011; see also Chapter 8). More broadly, ethics and values can also have a significant influence on the construction of social workers' identities, both individual and collective, as we will see in Chapter 7. From interviewing various social work informants, as well as considering the findings of other published research, it appears that practitioners may be concerned about a lack of possibilities for exercising their judgement in ways that are acceptable to them as professionals (see, for example, Papadaki and Papadaki, 2008). In a previous publication (Bell, 2015), I considered the significance of ethics and values to the construction of social work identity/ies, and while I concluded that these identities are inevitably fragile and contested, Chandler's (2017: 166, emphases in the original) recent discussion of identity at work adds another strand to these arguments by suggesting how related concepts of identification can be used:

> What exploration of *identification-with* leads to, potentially, is an uncovering of the connections that are made and the value that they have to the person making them. On the other hand, an exploration of *identification-of* allows us to explore how the person accounts for themselves ... [for example,] in processual, dialogic terms.

These suggestions resonate with the idea that we can demonstrate how social workers may be *identifying with* their clients/service users empathetically, while simultaneously accounting for themselves in various ways. Incorporating this approach allows us to examine in detail, in this and subsequent chapters, social workers' views about working with people, including 'their' 'clients'/'service users' (the use of language, including labels, being a salient point here), but also, in some cases, as part of their work as educators, with social work students. This should help to reveal the importance that social workers attach to instilling necessary changes into people's lives by working with them to transform and 'address life challenges and enhance wellbeing' (International Federation of Social Workers (IFSW), definition 2014). From an anthropological perspective, it is important to again make clear that I am exploring these issues not only through published literature, but also through my own direct contacts and interviews with particular social workers; as Hockey (2002) has suggested, this can form a kind of ethnographic exploration (to set alongside any actual ethnographic and auto-ethnographic work also reported here).

As we saw in Chapter 5, students undertaking social work education build their sense of professional identity gradually, often in collaboration with other students and with their educators/tutors. As Terum and Heggen (2016: 851)[1] found in their statistically based, Norwegian study of students' identification with social work, this identification seemed to come early on in the students' professional education:

> teacher–student interaction and interaction with supervisors at placement affects professional identification. Students who experience support and feedback from teachers and who have confidence in the supervisors' competence express a stronger dedication to and identification with the profession. This indicates, in accordance with previous research, that feedback from teachers and supervisors and the experience of good role models are important in professional socialization.

In a previous publication bringing together research and experiences from Denmark, Norway and England (Bell et al, 2017: 49), I and my co-authors discussed how we came to the conclusion that building a professional identity is a 'lifelong process of learning, acting and reflecting in education and practice'; this is a process that requires experience, analytical reflection and, in particular, time. We decided that building an identity is not only about knowledge acquisition, but also about the development of attitudes and experiences, and having the time to reflect on them. It was noticeable that in the country-based projects that we drew upon for that publication (see Bell and Villadsen, 2011), social work students tended to see their education as being outside reality and also seemed to be highly focused on social work practice, which seemed more 'real' to them, possibly as a key source of identity construction. However, according to one of my recently interviewed, experienced social worker/educator informants, there can be dangers in this way of forming a professional identity:

> '[With educational models] *that are shorter, the diploma, the Frontline programme, because what I think happens then is that*

their identity formation happens much more in practice, and we know that, and there's lots of research that says, practice is extremely varied from very good practice to extremely poor, proceduralised, managerialist practice ... and so that means that identity is formed in that setting, and we don't really want that. I think we want, as far as possible, people who really develop a certain independent identity when they go into practice.' (Transnational social worker/educator working in England in 2018)

In a similar vein, another English informant said that "*One of the biggest issues I've noticed in the last year is this emphasis on social workers in training doing statutory placements, which is where they get socialised into what the government thinks social work is.*" As we saw at the end of Chapter 5, according to many commentators, the integration of various elements, including not only theoretical knowledge, but also practice experience and the use of self,[2] does seem to be key to social workers developing their sense of individual identity, as well as to their competent practice (see Ruch, 2000; Butler et al, 2007; Gordon and Dunworth, 2017).

When carrying out my own research through interviews, I found that asking social workers about 'identity' provided an opportunity for them to reveal their perspectives on what it means to be a professional social worker. This line of enquiry could show me how they account for themselves, as well as suggesting how they prioritise certain aspects of their professional work. I interviewed the following social worker/educator, for example, a few years ago when I was investigating the relevance of evidence-based practice and professional identity (see Bell, 2008) and he explained how he had arrived at his current position:

'*I started out with a straightforward, purely academic, non-professional academic career ... that was up to PhD level* [in social sciences], *but for personal reasons, in terms of earning money, I ended up working part time in social care, and then it made sense that if I were to get professionally qualified in social work, I would have more opportunities, in social work itself ... in terms of direct practice, I've done about 15 years.... But, subsequently, what transpired was, having a PhD and a social work qualification, it was, there was an open door for me to go back into academia, to teach social workers.'* (Social worker/educator)

When asked to identify and 'account for' himself in relation to his current social work position, this same informant said he now chose to identify primarily as 'a social work teacher':

Informant: *'I'm trying to do everything I've got to help the students learn to be competent in* [their jobs], *so what would I describe myself as? I say, I'm a social work teacher, that's what I say to people when I meet them socially. If they say, "Where do you work?" I say, "I work at a university", if they say, "Oh, have you ever been a social worker?", I say, "Yes, and I'm still partly funded by a social work agency, which is very important to me actually, in terms of my links with people. But, in terms of saying "How would I describe myself?", I've never come up with a particularly snappy phrase.'*

Interviewer: *'That's your identity, you're a social work teacher?'*

Informant: *'I'm a social work teacher, yes.'*

Next, this social work manager, who was working in an intervention-based (non-statutory) service[3] when I interviewed her for an evidence-based practice and professional identity project, illustrates how language may be key to constructing not only the social worker's own sense of identity, but also their identity as others see them. This example also picks up Chandler's point about 'identification with' (others) being different from how individuals may account for themselves ('identification of'):

'We'll send out a calendar [for clients] *with our faces on, our titles on, but what* [does] *it actually mean?... And another family, when* [colleague] *was introduced to them as a "Parenting Practice Manager",* [they] *said, "What does that mean?" So, on the one hand, we say, "Yes, we've sent out the information", but we don't necessarily know whether the people have grasped what we're trying to do. A "Parenting Practice Manager", that's our language, not theirs. So, simple little things like that, and we learn from it, "Okay, we've got to do something about that."'* (Social work manager with 20+ years of experience, working in England)

Another recently interviewed social worker, currently employed in university social work education, recognised and celebrated her diverse sense of professional identity, including work as a practitioner and educator, while acknowledging its difficulties and limitations:

'I've been qualified for nearly 30 years – pre-qualifying as well – so I see it as something through time. So, I spent 14 years doing almost nothing but practice, then I spent a lot of time learning

how to be a teacher; occasionally, I dipped back into practice and have done some of that, but, of course, I have done research on top of all of that, so I see myself as having ... three aspects. And, although, in a sense, it waters it down because I can't say I'm any one of those singularly, defining it for me is in holding all of those because I find all of those aspects interesting. And it's a double-edged sword because it's fascinating, being able to go into each of them, but it means that you never seem to shine in any one of them really because you're not like the teacher, par excellence, because you're always thinking, "How can I use these ideas in practice and research?" There's a strength to it, but also, you know....' (Social worker/educator interviewed in 2018)

By interviewing social workers who had had experiences of working in different (organisational) settings, I found it interesting to see how far they managed to maintain or enhance what they thought of as their identity as a social worker. This was not always an easy process, but often seemed to rely on the worker's own values and approach to their work. For example, the following social worker, with experience of working with other professionals in multidisciplinary teams (MDTs) in the mental health field, suggested ways of enhancing her sense of identity as a social worker in this particular context:

'*You very much have to, as a social worker, earn the professional respect: that unless you are seen as someone competent and as someone who is knowledgeable and as someone who perhaps somewhat thinks like a doctor, that you are not going to be respected as much or considered I think, overall. So it's done in a very subtle way, but, you know, oftentimes, a lot of the social workers in MDTs complain that maybe when they speak to the doctor, it moves onto something else or, you know, it's done in very subtle formalities that, you know, you can't really overtly pick it up. But I think that you have to endeavour as a social worker in MDTs, especially within an adult setting, that you have to endeavour to work hard, and once you achieve respect from your peers and your colleagues ... your role is valued and considered. But I think that comes with practice and experience.*'

Working in this (mental health) context in England could involve being seconded to a health trust instead of being directly employed by the local authority, as this informant explained. This might mean, for example, that while continuing training opportunities could appear in either setting, it might also happen that these could be missed if "*you're a person seconded to* [the trust] *and so then, therefore, you fall in-between certain gaps*".

Another social worker who had qualified outside the UK spoke about her experiences of working in the UK voluntary sector:

Interviewer:	'*The voluntary sector, would you say, was that very different to working in local authorities, or what do you think?*'
Informant:	'*Well, my role was very different. The experience of working in that* [voluntary] *organisation was different because I wasn't doing statutory social work and in Britain, in England, if you are doing social work, the emphasis is on seeing that as statutory social work. So, you've got some kind of statutory role that you are undertaking. That is really different from other countries and how the social work role and the profession is organised. The government in this country has a hell of a say on what social work looks like, which is interesting in itself. I'm not criticising that, I'm just saying that's how it is here. In the voluntary sector, it's different and the role that I had was very much supporting statutory sector colleagues to do their work. So, we were coming in, doing some of the work that supported statutory sector colleagues that they didn't have time to do in detail.*'

This example also illustrates how the position of the state can influence not only policy, but also social workers' roles and, by extension, their views about their collective professional identity/ies. Some social workers that I talked to indicated that they felt a key part of that identity, strongly linked to their values, was in 'bringing people together'. Yet, this perspective could also be misunderstood, and there might also be a feeling that other professionals seem to have a more visible sense of *their* own identities:

'*I'm concerned about social workers' discipline and how we get misunderstood and occupied, really taken over, but partly for the reasons I've said: that we're not egotistical; we're actually about getting others to join together. And most people who are social workers, with the identity we have are very passionate about it, but it's very difficult to put into words because it comes from a very deep level of making it about fairness and social justice, and you'll find a lot of people have that as something personal, rather than professional, as well.'*

Another social worker discussed these unspoken aspects of identity recognition; later in her interview, she related this to earlier ways of working in which she felt there was *"more of a flexibility and discovery process in the way in which you did your work"*:

'*I think the idea of having a professional identity and how it's conceptualised now is different to the, what I think of as a, social work identity. So, although I act professionally and, um, you know, I remember when I was working as a social worker, language was so important, the way you spoke to people, the way you presented yourself. There were always boundaries you never crossed, but you would never say to somebody, "Oh, those boundaries were known", but they weren't, they didn't have to be articulated. So, you always had this sense of professionalism, but you never spoke much about your professional identity and it's been interesting actually to think about when, at what point in the development of social work, since I've been, since the eighties, did professional identity become such a big thing and I suppose it's to do with the regulation ... so it must have come when the degree started and then social work started to be regulated that people then started talking about professionalism, professional identity. But I still think that we had a very strong professional identity, but we didn't articulate it.'* (Social worker/educator interviewed in 2018)

Later, in Chapter 8 ('Relating and partnering'), I discuss further the project in which we explored social work students' views about the characteristics of various professions and occupations, including their own (see Bell and Allain, 2011). In this, they rated themselves highly on 'inter-professional skills' and being a 'team player', but less highly on 'leadership abilities' and 'confidence'. This gives us some indication of how social work students may view their own identities and how these compare with those of other professionals.

In these examples, it is clear how far both national and local policy contexts can shape the social worker's role on the ground, and yet I was also impressed by all my informants' collective allegiance to their profession and to its values and commitments (which we will discuss further in Chapter 7).

The professional 'stranger': still an outsider?

At this stage in the book, I feel that it would be good to also reflect on my own sense of professional identity as someone who has worked alongside social workers as a teacher and researcher. I already indicated that I have had some challenges to overcome in trying to establish my own identity when working in a social work academic context. Following on from my first foray into social work research, and having previously spent some years doing information work in academic and government libraries, I moved forward into an academic and teaching career. To begin with, little seemed to change as I became predominantly an academic teacher and (when opportunities arose) a researcher.[4]

As time went by and I worked more directly with social work students and staff who were or had been social workers, I became used to people, both inside and outside academia, saying to me, 'Oh, I always thought *you were* a social worker'. In fact, there were many occasions after taking up academic posts when my professional identity as a social worker was simply assumed. This has been awkward on occasions, but it has perhaps become less so since social work in England had achieved its protected title. This might seem paradoxical but it then became a simple matter of stating 'I am not registered as a social worker with the HCPC' – less ambiguity, so less chance of misunderstanding?. This was not always the case, and my attempts to avoid being identified with the profession that I have always found fascinating were also labelled as being about disloyalty on occasion, or even unwillingness on my part to undertake necessary work for my academic department.

When working as a lecturer in academia, I was happy to teach social worker students (especially within my own teaching specialism of research methodology, but also in the broader social sciences); I was also keen to supervise student projects and dissertations, as well as to carry out social work-related research. My 'teaching identity' was, of course, something that I shared easily with my social worker colleagues, though, as previously stated by one of my interview informants, there could be some issues about balancing this diversity of roles between teaching, research and (if you were a professional practitioner) your role as a social worker. However, research projects did give me an occasional, explicit chance to 'do anthropology', mostly through interviewing but sometimes through observational methods.

As a personal example of my own kind of necessary balancing, Box 6.1 contains an extract from observational notes that I took when working on the tutor groups project already discussed in earlier chapters (taken from Bell and Villadsen, 2010: 20–1).

Box 6.1: Observational notes[5] taken during the tutor groups research project

[Group has been discussing placements & student self-evaluative reports [part of student assessment] It is towards the end of the session. Observer (LB) is sitting to one side out of the group circle.]

Tutor asks the students what they would like to do next semester in the tutor group as they have been very focused on getting everyone started on their placements. A female student says she's really worried about the research proposal [which is part of the assessed work for my [the researcher's] methods module]. Several students turn to look directly at me [researcher]. I feel I must intervene (although I am not supposed to 'participate' in the group during the observation) and speak up to say that dealing with the research proposal is going to be covered in the first session of the research methods module next semester. The tutor then comments that she is OK about covering this topic in general but she does not want this [tutor] group to become a 'research seminar'. She then mentions work that was already done in the group in relation to another taught module. I resume my observation.

I felt able (as we saw in a previous chapter) to help with student recruitment or other activities that were close to the practice side of social work, provided that other academics who were qualified social workers were also on hand. Nevertheless, I have already indicated that looking back on my behaviour on some occasions does make me feel somewhat guilty, as if I felt that I was in danger of letting people down. The incident described in Box 6.1 did make me feel uncomfortable, though the tutor did not make any adverse comments afterwards.

I always had a clear idea of the areas of work that I felt were inappropriate for a non-social worker to undertake. Real sticking points for me came with areas such as the sole supervision of student (work) placements, or in having direct contact with educators based in practice settings relating to those students ; my consistent refusal to take on sole responsibility for student tutor groups and placements in this context also earned me some criticism from colleagues. Attempts on my part to move into a different academic department away from social work when the pressures became too great were refused by management. For quite a long time, I went about in academia saying firmly to people "well, of course I am *not a social worker*", which was noticed and commented on, especially by those who were not, themselves, social workers either! Yet, I felt sure that I ought to be helping to maintain professional standards by making sure that, as an outsider, I did not take on unwarranted responsibility for students' practice-based education; this should be left to the professionals. Did I revere social work professionals and their professional experiences too much? Possibly. I often wondered what exactly it was that they derived from their professional education/socialisation that I really lacked. There must be something! I felt sure that I was missing that something. Should I have tried harder to absorb a more obvious 'social work' identity? But how was I going to be able to do that since I had never experienced working with service users; to me, they were just people! Or, when (stubbornly) maintaining my own sense of professional identity (as 'a researcher'), was I expressing what I suspected that 'they' were thinking about me – that I was pushing my 'outsider' identity in their faces?[6]

This argument also raises the question of whether I was, in fact, 'doing ethnography' with the social workers and other colleagues on a day-to-day basis throughout my work as a lecturer. Although I accept that my anthropological background has shaped my ways of thinking or acting (see, again, Good, 1994), my overall purpose at that stage in my career was to be a lecturer and researcher, not an ethnographer day to day. It was only once I was coming to the end of my teaching career that I made the decision to step back and review my career, which has turned it all into a kind of 'ethnography', a narrative dialogue between myself and social workers (as noted in earlier chapters, see Barnard, 2000: 177).

Gradually, I think it dawned on me that the social workers I worked with just saw me as a person and fellow teacher/lecturer, precisely because they prided themselves on their own ability to get close to people and make good use of their own selves and emotions. They wanted to break down barriers and get close; but this also suggested to me that they wanted to somehow absorb me into 'their group'. I found this sometimes intrusive – it could even be upsetting – but it also reminded me of my own general reluctance to engage in 'their' use of self and way of being. My way of working was, I felt, to be professional and therefore impartial – somehow rational – and to resist becoming what I sometimes (still) regard as being overemotional (see Howe, 2008: 3–5). When feeling in a positive mood, I could even joke with non-social worker colleagues about how social workers would always seem to ask me 'And how do you *feel* about that?' However, being expected to work (it appears) more overtly with my emotions in a professional role has remained a sore point with me (but on exploring emotions in anthropological fieldwork, see, for example, Davies and Spencer, 2010; Beatty 2013). This is despite having been sometimes praised by social work colleagues for my ability to calm anxious students, and despite not being sure how I actually do that! A key question here should perhaps be not so much 'Was I rejecting the use of emotions as a professional approach?' (yes, I probably was), but 'Did it feel okay for me to do that?' (in social work contexts, no it didn't).

On the other hand, if preferring to see my own identification as being with other researchers, such as anthropologists, perhaps I was trying to make up for a feeling of being cut off from those fellow professionals by keeping my distance from social work (Sharland, 2012). Over the years, I continued to work with as many different kinds of students as I could (especially those on professional courses), but this also reflected my wish to seem collaborative and to bring people together (something that social work informants have said that they also do). Paradoxically, despite my continuing interest in inter-professional and multi-agency work, this has never meant that I favour a watered-down or blended version of professionalism; I do not believe that, in general, the social workers that I have recently spoken to want to be part of this blending either. For myself, to fit in 'nowhere' was better, I often felt, than forcing myself into the wrong space.

This is surely a perennial dilemma for any anthropologist; we may feel that we cannot be living and working 'at home' if we engage with any kind of anthropological work. We are trained to think of ourselves as outsiders, as 'professional strangers', and we act in this way in a bid to understand others; could this also be seen as a variant of what social workers try to do? Other professionals from health or social sciences were happy for me to teach their students research methods unproblematically (so, to some of them, I became a methodologist); but they did not usually try to absorb me into their disciplinary group(s), or at least not without acknowledging our professional differences!

Another link that I have always maintained is with feminist researchers and groups, and as the years passed, I published various book chapters and other work in that sphere with those colleagues. This is generally well within my comfort zone, where I feel 'at home'. Probably dating from the time of a sabbatical visit that I made with colleagues to the Middle East on a feminist-related project, I also began to see the tide turning for me in terms of how I was able to view my own sense of identity. I returned from the sabbatical and decided that I had to begin to work harder to make myself indispensable to the social work colleagues in my department, through both my teaching and research projects. In short, I wanted to feel 'at home'. By this time, my personal contacts were also becoming stronger, with, I feel, respect and acceptance on both sides. More recent forays to other European countries, including visits to international conferences, have shown me that elsewhere, where there is no protected title of 'social worker', it may also be easier to blend in with other people who are interested in social work and social work research from both insider and outsider perspectives; sure enough, on occasions, I have met other anthropologists, who must have always been there and were probably trying to / not to 'fit in' like me!

More recently, reviewing my work in social work, feminist research and research methodologies, including my interest in ethics (acquired along the way mainly through my work with students), has enabled me to reconsider my own sense of identity; so, I have been able (at last) to reflect on all my experiences for this book as 'an anthropologist'. At this point, and returning to Chandler's definition, I can much more confidently suggest that while I am now able to *identify with* social workers, I account for myself with an *identification of* being a researcher and an anthropologist; for me, this is a good compromise.

Chapter 6 summary

In this chapter, I have explored issues of identity for social workers, including how far there may be multiple or overlapping identities within social work, for example, practitioner/educator, when working with other professionals or in different sectors. The chapter ends with my own personal reflections on my identity as an 'outsider' to social work. In Chapters 7 and 8, we develop these ideas by exploring social workers' values and their relationships and partnerships with others in more detail.

Notes

[1]   For a discussion of a systematic review in this field, see also Heggen and Terum (2017).

[2]   See, for example, Butler, Ford and Tregaskis, C. (2007: 282), who argue that 'the use of self in relationship building should continue to be central to a profession such as social work'.

[3]   This manager had previously worked in 'statutory' services, for example, child protection, as well as with adults, but was currently working in a

parallel family service offering more in-depth intervention that followed up on referrals from other (statutory) social workers in the local authority.

[4] I have previously written about some of these earlier experiences in Bell and Birch (2007).

[5] One of my methods in this project was to observe a selection of actual tutor group meetings and try to make unobtrusive notes, rather than record the dialogue electronically, for confidentiality reasons. However, focus groups held with volunteer students as part of this research project were recorded. Ethics approval was obtained for both methods, as well as for staff interviews.

[6] See, for example, Sharland (2012: 215), citing the anthropologist Marilyn Strathern (2007), who suggests: 'Researchers who do venture across disciplinary boundaries all too easily find themselves intellectually and culturally "homeless"; they may face resistance, even ostracism, as neither one of "us" nor "them".'

Valuing and transgressing

Social workers frequently articulate the significance of their values to their professional identity/ies, collective and individual, as we saw in previous chapters. There have been many recent examinations of values and how these are (said to) underpin social workers' and other health- and social-care professionals' practice (see, for example, Hugman, 2005; Banks, 2012; Bell and Hafford-Letchfield, 2015). As we have already seen in earlier chapters, some commentators (for example, Clark, 2006) suggest that social work should be defined as a 'moral' activity, at least partly dependent on social workers' own character(s) (see also Bisman, 2004; Holmström, 2014). Frequently mentioned values include commitments to taking action (often with other professionals) on behalf of disadvantaged or vulnerable people; for social workers specifically, professional commitments towards social justice (including equality and fairness) and human rights are significant (see, for example, O'Brien, 2011; Higgs, 2015). Some of my interviewees suggested, for example, that being non-judgemental was also important; an example given to me recently was of a social worker being inappropriately judgemental of a service user who was living in poverty and asking for a crisis loan by responding with the suggestion that she should first 'turn off her television' (presumably to save money).

I have identified a number of publications, for example, setting out the challenges of working effectively with communities in a globalised context (see, for example, Gray et al, 2008; Healey, 2008; Healey and Link, 2011). However, it seems to me that it is often difficult to pin down how social work values in support of social justice are translated into actual professional practice (see O'Brien, 2011; see also Chapter 8). Similarly, as we have already identified in Chapter 5, for example, there is a wider debate among social workers about how to link professional theory with practice, which is equally difficult to pin down.

Several of my recently interviewed informants were keen to discuss social work values, and all of these informants linked these to issues of social justice. For example, the following English social worker/educator who qualified in the 1980s said:

'*I … think that our social work values, as highlighted in things like the International Federation of Social Work's definition, are a lot about social justice. And that leaves us, and this therefore comes into an issue for social workers if they choose to take it up, is that we often occupy a rather awkward space because we work for the government and, of course, we must work within the law; and we work for local authorities within a hierarchy and we must follow policy and procedure, and yet some of the kind of the current thinking seems to me, and the changes in legislation around the [financial] benefits etc, don't really promote social justice, don't really promote empowerment and therefore it leaves social workers in quite a difficult position.*'

This quotation also links us once again to the overarching idea that social workers must not only care, but at the same time, be prepared to control. Another social worker that I interviewed in 2018 agreed that maintaining a commitment to social justice was very challenging and would need to be addressed head on, requiring creative social work and also positive leadership:

'*Social justice, it's about the transformative potential that social work can offer families and that when you place that at the centre of your service, then there's a lot that is possible. So, I don't want to create this picture of doom and gloom and say, "Oh, you know, it's all going to be terrible." I think it's going to be really challenging and we need to be teaching the social workers, who are coming through our programmes, to be as creative as they possibly can, to understand what evidence is, how to apply that, but to also do what they can with what they've got and to, for people who are moving into leadership positions, to be able to create good cultures within organisations and to just not forget why they are there, who their service users are and to really meet those challenges head on.*'

A third English social worker whom I recently interviewed described how she saw the current social, economic and political context exacerbating issues of social justice, as well as professional values, when working on the front line:

'*I think when you've got a profession that is in, in a time of austerity, where you've got high [eligibility] threshold levels, so only priority cases are worked with, they've got higher caseloads, they are fire-fighting, they're dealing with urgent needs. They are not able to work in a preventative way, so they're doing short-term solutions that are leading to increased demand in the longer run, rather than, you know, working in a way that might prevent tragedies and crises coming forth. So, I think that's difficult for social work, individual social workers and their organisations, so I think it's a really difficult time to be a service user or a carer.'*

While social workers do appear to share values such as a commitment to social justice across countries and cultures, there is also some evidence that such values may differ, especially in terms of how 'service users' are viewed. For example, Hatton (2001, cited in Bell, 2015: 45) compares the value bases of social workers in the UK and in Denmark, suggesting that the former are more likely to recognise differences between users of services than their Danish colleagues, where social solidarity and equality are instead emphasised. This has implications for challenging discrimination (for another example of how this approach plays out in practice in Denmark, see Antoft et al, 2017).

At the time of writing this book, the Health and Care Professions Council (HCPC) has been the regulatory body covering *English* social work since August 2012; this is in addition to their regulation of some other professions allied to health and social care. Since 'social worker' is now a protected title in England, social workers need to be registered with the HCPC in order to actively work in the profession in England (there are parallel regulatory bodies for Scotland, Wales and Northern Ireland). The HCPC is responsible for regulating social work and other professions by: setting standards for those registered ('registrants'); approving the professional educational programmes that they need to undertake; and checking on the fitness to practise of social workers or other professionals who appear not to have met professional standards. The HCPC website pointed out in 2018 that fitness to practise is not just about professional performance (of their 'registrants'), but also concerns issues of public confidence in the relevant profession. Similar HCPC standards are meant to apply across all their registered professions.

Turning the issue of social work values around, I wondered what an examination of the very detailed and public fitness-to-practise hearings held by the HCPC Competence and Conduct Committee could add to our understanding of social work values. Would I be able to understand which values social workers seemed to be transgressing, as revealed by these fitness-to-practise materials? How were these transgressions addressed? Previous research on the General Social Care Council (GSCC) and subsequently the HCPC conduct hearings by

McLaughlin and colleagues (McLaughlin et al, 2016; McLaughlin, 2010; Worsley et al, 2017), including interviews with social workers, has demonstrated the (often negative) effects that fitness-to-practise hearings can have on individuals and their careers; this research also suggests some flaws as well as strengths in these organisational and regulatory processes.

As part of my explorations into social work values for this chapter, I therefore carried out a small (unfunded) project during 2018 to further examine what kinds of values appear to be relevant to these HCPC hearings, and I tried to examine how these issues are responded to by practitioners and the regulatory body itself (restricting my analysis to HCPC social worker registrants only[1]).

Fitness to practise in social work: an exploration

I examined the publicly available (online) HCPC documentation about recent hearings related to registered social workers (registrants) during 2017 (from January to December), and carried out a closer examination of the first 100 cases concerning individual social work practitioners. I have excluded detailed examination of the smaller number of cases coming before the Health Committee (some of which are held in private) and I concentrated on hearings from the Competence and Conduct Committee, although there is sometimes overlap between the individuals whose conduct is addressed by hearings held by the Health Committee.

My method involved reviewing all the social work cases coming before the HCPC's Competence and Conduct Committee in 2017 and sorting out categories of cases by gender and outcome ('striking off' the register or other results), as well as noting where cases were dismissed ('not well found'), where 'no further action' was taken following a hearing or where the registrant had voluntarily agreed to be removed from the register.

Examination of the first 100 cases not only illustrated the transgressions of each registrant in detail, providing what might be termed as a 'process recording' of the hearing, but also described the deliberations of the committee itself regarding the proposed outcome of the case. These deliberations are not specifically my focus here, except where they might illustrate examples of values. Decisions can include deciding whether various outcomes are sufficient or not for this particular case (especially for matters of public protection), and they seem to progress in a kind of hierarchy going from 'no further action', to 'caution', to 'interim suspension', (full) 'suspension' or 'conditions of practice' (where details may be specified and/or conditions are set for a certain period with regular reviews thereafter). Finally, the sanction may become 'striking off' the register; this can sometimes happen immediately after a first hearing following what is considered to be a very serious offence, or striking off may come much further down the line for the individual following a long series of hearings, suspensions or other sanctions. I did come across one registrant who was reinstated having earlier been struck off by the previous social worker registration body, the GSCC.

To provide some background for my project results, we need to first consider how many social workers there are currently registered in England and then how many come before the HCPC committees: the most recent HCPC statistics showed that 93,872 social workers were currently registered (registrants) with the HCPC in England at the time of writing this book (in June 2018). Of these, 76,957 (81.9 per cent) were women and 16,914 (18 per cent) were men. One person was registered with an undisclosed gender.

My examination of the records of the recent hearings for 2017 showed that 270 individuals came before HCPC hearings at some time between January and December 2017 (166 women [61.5 per cent]; 104 men [38.5 per cent]). This represents a very small percentage of the total number of registered social workers based on the current figures indicated above (approximately 0.28 per cent); however, these current figures do not include those who had already been struck off during 2017, which might slightly reduce this percentage. We can also see that proportionately more men than women registrants came before the committee (given the overall numbers, by gender, registered with the HCPC). These are relatively small figures, yet this result is still striking.

Many individuals came before the Competence and Conduct Committee several times as their case was reviewed across the year, from a previous year or going into the next year in different hearings. So, for example, during the first five months of 2017 (while examining the first 100 cases), I found that 37 individuals (19 women and 18 men) had cases that were continuing over from 2016, or from earlier years 2014–16 in a few cases. Similarly, some of the 270 identified individuals had cases still under review going into 2018.

What were the outcomes for these registrants? For 62 individuals (33 women [53 per cent]; 29 men [43 per cent]) their cases ended with them being struck off the register during 2017 or in the early part of 2018. In addition, eight women and three men agreed to their voluntary removal from the register in the same period (this included some being removed for health reasons). This amounts to 27 per cent of the total 270 individuals coming before the HCPC Competence and Conduct Committee hearings that year.

During 2017, 191 individuals came before the HCPC hearings where there was considered to be a case to answer (120 women [63 per cent]; 71 men [37 per cent]). All these received lesser sanctions than striking off, including caution, (interim or full) suspension or 'conditions of practice' (where details may be specified and/or conditions are set for a certain period, with regular reviews thereafter). This amounts in total to 71 per cent of the original 270 cases. Many of these cases will therefore continue to be monitored going into 2018 and perhaps beyond.

Considering these outcomes in more detail, within *the first 100 cases* (over the five months of January to May 2017), my examination of these records showed that there were eight registrants (five women and three men [3 per cent of total]) whose cases ended in a caution. Four further cases (three women and one man) ended in no further action being taken following a full hearing. Two additional cases (both women) were considered to be not well founded and there was (presumably) no further investigation of these cases either (2 per cent of cases in total).

Some case examples

At this point, I needed to explore in a bit more detail why individuals seemed to have received specific sanctions, including being struck off. I give a few examples in the following section of how issues of values and professionalism could play out within this HCPC system, taking examples from my examination of the first 100 cases for 2017. I am being careful to maintain the confidentiality of individuals and organisations (including employers) when examining these records, although such details are, in fact, revealed publicly in the online records. I did find a few cases in which sanctions were imposed for moral reasons, such as the registrant conducting an inappropriate (sexual) relationship with a vulnerable service user ('in breach of policies on professional boundaries'); there were also a few criminal cases, such as someone having been convicted in a criminal court for dishonesty or being convicted of sexual assault/possession of child pornography. However, these kinds of rare examples were not my main focus.

The examples I discuss in the following section relate more specifically to an examination of the registrants' professional work as social workers and the more nuanced aspects of their transgression of various professional values, including breaches of confidentiality, failure to carry out allocated tasks or lack of competence when managing social work cases. In all cases, legal representation was involved in some way, as would be expected in these processes.

Example 1

In this case, a female social worker was accused of various failings in relation to her work with several separate families where there were 'children in need'. This amounted partly to a lack of competence in managing cases but also to serious misconduct in the sense that her line manager (who acted as a witness to the hearing) had given evidence that this misconduct was due to 'a combination of *wilful* action, and negligence' (emphasis added): in this case, misconduct included *breaches of confidentiality* and lack of competence in *assessing situations* and in *communicating* effectively. Evidence showed that this social worker had initially engaged with the HCPC over these matters but that she had not been in contact with them for more than one year by the final stage of the hearings process.

The final decision by the panel in this case (several years after the case was first heard) resulted in a 'striking off' order:

> The Panel went on to consider whether a period of suspension would be appropriate in this case. A period of suspension might have been appropriate if the Registrant had engaged with the process and demonstrated insight into her misconduct and lack of competence, such that there was not a significant risk of repetition, and that there were personal mitigating circumstances that demonstrated that these matters did not arise out of attitudinal problems. Unfortunately, that is not the case here. The Registrant has disengaged from the process, and has not provided any evidence of insight or remorse.

The apparently '*wilful*' nature of this social worker's actions, including her subsequent lack of engagement with the HCPC processes, thus seems to have tipped the balance over into a 'striking off' outcome.

Example 2

In this case, the social worker was first suspended due to a lack of competence or misconduct in relation to the management of several cases, involving issues such as failing to carry out tasks that she had been allocated. However, it was noted that she had a 'good work record, with no previous history of failings', and that 'the events occurred over a relatively short period of time in an otherwise lengthy career'. The social worker had identified that she had health issues at that time, and she subsequently took sick leave, which was noted. At the first full hearing, it was decided that a striking off order would be 'disproportionate', and so the registrant was instead suspended for a certain period.

Following a subsequent review of the case (at the next hearing), which the registrant did not attend, the panel said that they did not consider that these issues were minor or isolated, and they identified a risk of repetition. They noted that she had 'failed to engage with this review and not provided this panel with any of the evidence suggested by the previous panel'. The panel accepted the evidence of a witness that no actual harm had been identified to any of the service users in this case; 'however it was of the view that the failures of the Registrant had the potential to put them at risk of significant harm'.

At the final hearing, the panel decided to strike off the registrant from the social workers' register. In what seems to be a partial justification of this final review of the case, it was stated that:

> The purpose of fitness to practise proceedings is not to punish registrants, but to protect the public. There is a public interest in upholding the reputation of the profession and maintaining public confidence in the HCPC Regulatory process. In deciding what, if any, sanction to impose under Article 29 of the Health and Social Work Professions Order 2001, the Panel has had regard to the principle of proportionality and the need to balance the interests of the public with those of the Registrant, in accordance with the advice of the Legal Assessor.

Example 3

In a third example, resulting in a final 'caution' outcome (imposed for the standard three years), there was unauthorised access to records that were focused upon confidential child protection cases, where the registrant personally knew the people involved. The registrant had therefore breached the HCPC's standards of conduct, performance and ethics with respect to two specific standards: '3 You must respect the *confidentiality* of service users'; and '13 You must behave with ...

integrity and make sure that your behaviour does not *damage the public's confidence* in you or your profession' (emphases added).

There were a number of interesting features to this case that clearly affected the outcome: the registrant was newly qualified; he cooperated fully with the enquiry; and he attended the hearing. Although the final judgement was that his fitness to practise remained 'impaired' through 'misconduct', he provided oral evidence to the hearing and had also written a detailed reflective piece that was taken into account. Furthermore, the panel found that evidence provided by a witness to the hearing was 'of limited assistance'. In addition, it was noted that the registrant felt unsupported by his managers, but through his oral evidence and written reflection, he accepted his own misconduct and showed remorse.

Example 4

In this example, the male registrant was made subject to 'conditions of practice' as he was considered to have breached several of the HCPC's standards of proficiency for social workers in England, specifically:

> 8.11 – be able to prepare and present formal reports in line with the applicable protocols and guidelines....
> 9.7 – be able to contribute effectively to work undertaken as part of a multi-disciplinary team....
> 10.1 – be able to keep accurate, comprehensive and comprehensible records in accordance with applicable legislation, protocols and guidelines.

This was a complex case continuing over several years, during which time the registrant had been subject to specific 'conditions of practice': he was able to continue to work with children in need and with looked-after children but not allowed to work as a social worker in child protection. The panel considered a number of allegations made against the registrant in addition to those breaches listed earlier; not all of the allegations could be proved according to the evidence that was presented to the hearing (by more than one witness). He remained under supervision with respect to, in particular, following management instructions, workload management and recordkeeping. The panel also noted at one stage that what was termed a 'clash of personalities' with the registrant's manager was part of the overall picture. The panel considered that 'given the Registrant's insight and continued engagement, conditions of practice could be formulated which would adequately protect the public and assist in the Registrant achieving full remediation'.

Example 5

As a final example, a registrant with many years of social work experience who had been subject to 'conditions of practice' asked for an early review of his case as he was keen to be reinstated as a registered social worker. He was subject to conditions and supervision, particularly in relation to recordkeeping, following procedures and risk assessment. He stated that he had been unable to obtain a professional social work post with these conditions of practice in place. The registrant had engaged with the HCPC process and had been employed in a social care role since the previous hearing. At this hearing, the panel understood that he would like to be employed as a social worker, both for financial reasons and because he considered that he had a 'calling' to do social work. However, the panel stated that because this was an early review, 'there is a burden of persuasion upon the Registrant'. The panel was not satisfied that he had provided sufficient evidence that the 'conditions of practice' had been met; as a result, his 'conditions of practice' remained in place until the time planned for the end of the restriction. The panel were unconvinced that a restriction was no longer required for the protection of service users and for the wider public interest.

These selected examples illustrate the complexities involved in regulatory HCPC fitness-to-practise hearings and suggest how professional values and, indeed, wider issues of ethics underpin these cases. In some cases, where clear moral issues were exposed (for example, of dishonesty), this would certainly bear out some of the arguments made by those emphasising the importance of social workers' moral character (Bisman, 2004; Clark, 2006; Holmström, 2014). However, this was why I did *not* focus only on such examples, but looked in more detail at the more ambiguous cases instead. Breaches of formal standards are certainly part of the picture, as detailed in the five example cases, but so too are more personal issues, such as those defined as 'personality clashes'. It is also interesting to see that gender may play a part in these processes, though it is not clear why this is. Why do proportionally more men than women registrants seem to appear before these hearings (compared to the overall gender profile of those registered with the HCPC)? Do men and female social workers react in different ways to being brought before the committee?

For example, despite very small numbers, we can see that in 2017, a few more women than men agreed to their own voluntary removal from the HCPC register. It is difficult to explain all this without resorting to gender stereotyping, for example, in relation to gendered personality traits. Perhaps there are also examples where managers or workers come into conflict, and this can lead to an initial reporting to the HCPC (see Examples 1 and 4).

I am also mindful here of McLaughlin, Leigh and Worsley's (2016) discussion, which suggests that particular outcomes from HCPC competence and conduct hearings may relate not only to the transgressions of individuals, but also to contextual issues of workload, employer's supervision and so on. However:

> The focus of the HCPC proceedings is on the action and behaviour of the *individual social worker* ... this represents a key difference between such hearings and serious case inquiries. The latter certainly provide a narrative and moral judgment about the conduct of professionals but, crucially, they also consider organisational factors that may have impacted on practice. In contrast, HCPC hearings are predominantly focused on the actions and behaviour of the individual registrant. (McLaughlin et al, 2016: 385, emphasis added)

As my earlier examples illustrated, outcomes from hearings are also related to how individuals conduct themselves when challenged to explain their 'impaired' behaviour, as McGregor (2014: 386) also suggests: 'many of those social workers who are subject to the regulatory process from initial complaint to final outcome choose not to attend their fitness to practise hearing.... The reason for their absence is unknown'.

Examining the overall HCPC processes in relation to social work through these and other examples reveals how (or if) individuals actually engage with the regulatory body, and also sheds light on how the evidence of witnesses (and the HCPC panel's reactions to this evidence) can have a key role to play in hearings. I concur with McLaughlin, Leigh and Worsley's (2016) assessment that it is significant that the focus of the HCPC hearings tends to be on the action and behaviour of the *individual social worker*. This implies that while the hearings must be underpinned by a focus on individuals' compliance with particular standards, as illustrated here (such as maintaining confidentiality and upholding public confidence in the profession), this is not the whole story. These standards typically reflect *professional ethics*, and as Whittington and Whittington (2015: 81) point out, these 'are typically expressed in professional and regulatory codes and provide both guides to expected conduct and standards of accountability'.

We also need to explore how these (public protection) standards map onto social workers' values (both personal ['Moral'?] and collectively as a profession). One of my own recent interviewees, who said that she had had some professional involvement with HCPC regulatory processes, suggested that compared to other professions regulated by the HCPC organisation, social work seemed to be at a disadvantage; she thought that this was because social work did not currently have a professional body capable of taking forward big agendas regarding good practice, having to primarily rely instead on the HCPC's public protection standards as a 'baseline'.

Certainly, as we have seen in the case examples, the implications of relying on these standards appear complex. Despite an apparently individualised focus and implied links to social workers' personal and professional values, we have also seen from this exploration of fitness-to-practise hearings how organisational and social issues (including gender) may sometimes play a key part in how these hearings play out for individuals, especially in terms of professional outcomes.

New developments

At the time of writing this chapter, Social Work England is poised to take over the reins as regulator for all social workers in England from December 2019. A glance at their interim website reveals that they are a non-departmental public body (at arm's length from government) based in Sheffield, and their main stated objective 'will be to protect the public'. They describe themselves on their website as 'an independent public protection body, setting professional, education and training standards for social workers'.

There was a recent consultation on the new framework of appointment rules (for advisers, panels of advisers, investigators, case examiners, adjudicators and inspectors), which has been endorsed by the British Association of Social Workers (BASW). Social Work England is operating a further consultation period between February and April 2019. This consultation process is planned to involve a number of events in different areas of England, which:

> will focus on the rules and standards which we need to set
> before we can begin our work. This includes the standards

we have drafted for social workers and training providers, and the rules we are putting in place for how:
- social workers register with us.
- we deal with concerns raised about social workers.
- we approve social work courses with education and training providers.

To date, Social Work England has appointed a chair and board members, as well as an executive director of standards, and the plan is to appoint seven regional engagement leads. According to the executive director, the aim for the regulator is to be 'informed, authentic and collaborative', and her introduction (currently on the website) certainly conveys a sense of optimism and excitement about the launching of the new regulator. However, this is tempered with comments alluding to social work practice, stressing 'the impact it has when we get it wrong, and the difference it makes when we get it right'.

Chapter 7 summary

Social work values, such as promoting social justice, are considered key to this occupational group. Many of my interviewees seemed to share similar values; however, these values sometimes seem to vary culturally and geographically. International social work espouses additional values by placing an emphasis on globalisation and international development (for example, Healey, 2008). I am also concerned in this chapter with what happens when social workers fail to live up to their professional standards, and what sanctions may be applied. I have drawn upon published research as well as data from my own research into recent, publicly available material on social workers' processes of deregistration and other sanctions (see also, for example, Worsley et al, 2017). The chapter ends with a look ahead to the imminent establishment of the new social work regulator for England, Social Work England.

Note
[1] I am grateful to Professor Aidan Worsley for discussing with me his ongoing work with his colleagues (Ken McLaughlin and Sarah Shorrock) comparing fitness-to-practise proceedings for social workers and other health professionals.

Relating and partnering: social workers, clients/service users and other professionals

Relationships are important to all of us, but what about social workers? From my discussions so far, we can see that 'relationship' and 'relationships', as well as 'partnership(s)', are very important concepts to social work and social workers. In this chapter, I want to explore further what some of the social workers I interviewed say about these concepts, and how they explain their significance to social work. I will also draw upon some of my own social work-based research to illustrate 'relating' and 'partnering' in practice.

In Chapter 1, I acknowledged that, in very basic terms, some kind of relationship between those who provide social work and those who receive it is surely a (complex) cornerstone of all social work discourses and practices. This also implies the involvement of emotions, however those are defined or assessed (see, for example, Howe, 2008).[1] The relationships that social workers have with their service users or 'clients', their colleagues, other professionals, and any other people with whom they come into contact are surely an important part of the overall picture.

We would expect a focus on relationship(s) to apply in these professional contexts, but for those who have been motivated to train and to work in *social* work and related occupations, this concept may also resonate personally in ways that could be different from those who are not social workers. For example, we could ask whether social workers view emotions in particular ways? Beatty (2013) discusses the ways in which anthropologists have studied emotions in various settings; using examples mainly from what he terms 'traditional' social settings, he critically reviews whether researchers have been able to cross-culturally define what exactly emotions are.[2]

We have already seen in earlier chapters that the anthropologist Byron Good suggests that doctors construct a view of the body that 'sees' it differently from those who have not had medical training. Do those who have been educated and trained to construct particular (culturally based) views of relationship(s) and emotions (including social workers) therefore claim to understand them differently to other people? Does constructing a 'professional' view of relationship(s), informed by various levels of theory, provide someone with a deeper or more complete view? Or, alternatively, does holding such beliefs put barriers between professionals and those who have not been educated in this way? There are all kinds of possibilities here, including the idea that social work has tended to privilege Eurocentric understandings of psychology and emotional development (see, for example, Staeuble, 2006; Robinson, 2008). This is also to be understood in the context of social work seeming to be uncertain as a profession, especially when social workers are working within current neoliberal agendas (see, for example, Dickens, 2011; Chandler et al, 2015, 2017).

In this chapter, I also want to include the separate but linked concept of 'partnership'. Dickens (2010: 9) for example suggests that 'partnership working' is essential to 'break down barriers, promote joint planning and working', and ensure 'joined up solutions to joined up problems'. As Whittington and Whittington (2015: 76) have suggested: 'Although not all relationships are partnerships, all partnerships involve relationships'. Whittington and Whittington (2015: 77) (emphasis in original) also point out, no single definition prevails of what partnership is, with their own definition being as follows: '*Partnership* in social work represents an agreed, co-operative relationship, carrying explicit or implied rights or obligations and possible imbalances of power, which may be formed with service users and carers, and among and between teams, professionals and organisations; partnership is a particular state of relationship.' Whittington and Whittington (2015: 77) further define 'collaboration' as 'partnership in action' (see also Weinstein et al, 2003).

Examining some of the literature relating to these broad concepts of 'relationship' and 'partnership' reveals a myriad of discussions relevant to social work (see, for example, Douglas, 2008), both in books about 'how to do' social work (such as Payne, 2006; Hennessey, 2011; Coulshed and Orme, 2012; Thompson, 2015), and in publications focusing on more specific topics, such as what is defined as 'relationship-based practice' (see, for example, Megele, 2015; Bryan et al, 2016; Ruch et al, 2018; Dix et al, 2019). The idea that 'not all relationships are partnerships' implies some kind of power imbalance between social workers and those with whom they work, which, as we have already seen, stems from the idea that, in practice, social workers will need to control as much as to care (on 'power', see, for example, Hafford-Letchfield, 2015). Payne (2006: 60), for example, seeks to explain this complexity by suggesting that if we view social work as an intervention, then an implication is that 'the social order requirement for invoking social control is incorporated into the basic therapeutic approach of personal and interpersonal social work'. Payne sees the altruism of caring being balanced against the authoritative imposition of social work involvement. As I will discuss later, this issue is at the heart of debates about whether social workers can base their practice on relationships while also taking a person-centred approach (see Murphy et al, 2013).

Some of the social workers that I very recently interviewed talked explicitly about relationships and building partnerships, particularly with users of social work services. The following English informant, who is a social worker with many years of experience, explained to me how social workers need to use their relationship skills and their emotional intelligence to make sense of what is happening for their service users, while also understanding the relevance of the underpinning knowledge and theories that they have been taught to use:

Interviewer: 'It sounds like relationships and emotional intelligence, if you like, are very, you think that's very important for social work?'

Informant: 'I think that's massively important. I think that is the key to social work. If you haven't got that, the scholarly activity, academic theory, logical though that might be, that is not going to resonate with you when you're placed before somebody and you're having to read and pick up and analyse as you're going in front of them, what is happening. If you're not, if you haven't done that internal work, that's not going to work.'

Another experienced social worker discussed the complexity of working with people who have entrenched problems, and how this links to building a relationship with them:

'I think that ... particularly because we are driven to this statutory, very complex work ... it's not about bath aids, nine times out of ten, it's not something simple like that, and therefore I think one has to look at people's emotional world, as well as: is the world out there a level playing field and what are we doing to improve people's life chances? But in order to do that, I think you have to build a relationship, you know for people who have never had options.'

This same social worker went on to describe how relationship building can also be affected by more structural factors, such as consistency in the workforce:

> '*I think given that probably the majority of people we work with have those sorts of entrenched problems, you are looking at longer-term interventions where they can actually build trust in authority. So, they need social workers who are going to be consistent, who are going to stay ... you know, we have a real problem with social workers staying in the job, 50 per cent leave after five years, which means we're constantly chasing experience. But it also means that the service users are constantly being confronted with having to build a new relationship and, understandably, quite a number of them think, "We're not going to."*'

The two social workers that I have just quoted from were talking mainly about face-to-face contexts and their individual encounters with service users; however, the social workers I talked to clearly also saw that strategic approaches or overall 'ways of working' could be modelled on similar principles of relationship building. The following, third social worker describes an approach that could be put into practice, making good use of relationships with service users, and also involving other aspects of partnership. I was interested to hear from her that in current circumstances, while already implemented in some places, this model might be seen as innovative elsewhere and it was not necessarily dependent on funding:

> '[As an example of a recent initiative,] *a particular way of working in that [local] area, which places the relationship between social worker and service user at the centre of all the work that is done, and it's not about doing to people, but actually working with them and listening to them and engaging in relationship-based social work. So, I think there are some very good ideas and some very good models for how we can work well with the people who need social work services, even when faced with these appalling cuts to services, because money is not everything, it's a huge part of how we can work well, but it's not the only part. I think that one of the things that we need for the future is some very able strategic thinkers and good leaders to manage what we have to the best of our ability and who value what social work can become.*'

In a similar way, another experienced social worker/educator interviewed in England in 2018 described how she knew of one local area where:

> '*They're going back more to community-based work and asset-based approaches, which they are very open that that was borne out of austerity. They … say actually in terms of what they're doing, their social workers are liaising more in terms of community work and their strategy, and it's not always the social workers, you know, some of them are being held back to do high-risk work, but the strategy of the council is for the community to look after itself and be supported in doing so.*'

These kinds of approaches seem to imply situations where front-line social workers and their managers can make good use of their own professional judgement. Yet, as Perlinski, Blom and Evertsson (2017: 254) have suggested, whereas welfare professionals (including social workers) across Europe used to have a more central role in formulating and implementing welfare policies, the current role of the state in various welfare settings has changed: recently, 'welfare professions have experienced increased attempts to manage and control their professional practice. The welfare state is still very dependent on professions, but does not fully rely on their professional discretion.'

Basing social work practice on relationships

Despite their apparent loss of professional discretion, especially in what is termed 'statutory' work, relationship-based practice seems to remain significant to social workers. Several recent texts, including those by Megele (2015), Ruch, Turney and Ward (2018) and the forthcoming book by Dix, Hollinrake and Meade (2019), all encourage social workers to take up this kind of approach. As Megele (2015: 6, emphasis added) suggests: 'a collaborative and co-productive relationship-based approach to interventions with a psychosocial perspective and a reflective and effective *use of self* are foundational to empowering practice that can enable and maintain positive change'.

However, although social workers frequently discuss the empowerment of people with whom they work, it seems clear to an outsider that (certainly within statutory work) it is social workers (and, behind them, the state) who hold most of the power. Some authors, notably Murphy, Duggan and Joseph (2013), have debated the potential incompatibility of taking up a relationship-based approach with being fully person-centred. They argue persuasively that these two approaches are based on incompatible philosophical and theoretical underpinnings: the relationship is not an end in itself in a relationship-based approach, but developing it enables the professional to be 'persuasively directive in practice' (see Megele, 2015: 6); whereas being person-centred (derived from its own theoretical basis, as discussed by Murphy, Duggan and Joseph [2013]) implies that it is the relationship itself that is the key to unlocking the service user's own power over their future, without the professional being directive.

Taking this argument one stage further, I would argue that it is not always clear where the individual's power (whether that of a professional or a user of services) starts or ends. There may, for example, be an invocation of the rules (in order to be 'persuasively directive' and ensure compliance on the part of the professional; or alternatively in order to try and ensure their rights on the part of the users of services themselves). Sometimes, these perspectives seem to me to come into conflict. I can best illustrate this point briefly with reference to one of my own experiences that happened while I was working alongside university-based social workers (see Box 8.1).

Box 8.1: Following the rules

The importance to social workers of following the rules was brought home to me in a conversation I once had with a senior social work colleague about student marking (assessment). It went something like this:

Colleague: *'Have you got the student grades from your course to give me?'*
Me: *'I'm really sorry, I have most of the grades but I am still waiting for X* [another colleague] *to give me her grades, I should receive these from her later this week.'*
Colleague: *'But you said you would hand me the grades by today.'*
Me: *'Yes, I'm really sorry but I need to get all the grades in to check, then I can give them all to you at the same time.'*
Colleague: *'But you are the course leader, you promised me all the grades by today.'*
Me: *'Yes, I know, I thought X would have given me the grades before now, I will have to ask her again, I'm sorry.'*
Colleague: *'But you promised ...'*
Me: *'*[Getting irritated.] *Yes, I know, but ...'*
Colleague: *'I really can't understand why you cannot give me your grades today.'*

I reflected afterwards that my irritation must be what service users sometimes
feel like when faced with seemingly impossible social work(er) rules.

The difficulty of service users and others discussing 'the rules' with
professionals is something that is sometimes commented on; however,
some professionals seem to have made a good effort to enter into
such dialogues and thereby to reflect on their own power, even while
remaining directive (for example, on their work with parents in
Norway, see Seim and Slettebø , 2011; Slettebø, 2013; see also the
'Mothers Apart' partnership/action-based project that I describe later
in this chapter).

However, one of my recent interviewees pointed out to me (as we
noted earlier) that some areas of social work practice (such as group
work) are no longer considered as important as previously, and this
also seems to reflect changing policies in both social work education
and social work practice requirements:

Informant: '*I think it's a policy decision that group work is not a
                 requirement in any statutory setting. I can see, you know,
                 there's a focus primarily on assessments, on putting in
                 care packages and closing cases. So, essentially, it's part of
                 this whole care management system that was introduced
                 in the 1970s as well. So, the whole idea is not so much
                 about doing what social workers are meant to do, which
                 is to enable people, not only to resolve their immediate
                 difficulty that they might have, but actually to improve
                 their capacity, to the point where they are able to in future,
                 to avoid requiring help.*'

Interviewer: '*Yes, to be more independent?*'

Informant: '*Yes, to promote independence and to improve their
                 capacity for problem solving and all of that. I mean social
                 workers don't assume we have all the answers, but, at
                 the same time, if we can enable people to recognise that
                 they've got certain abilities that they can actually use
                 to improve their condition, at least to better than what
                 it was, then, in a sense, that is what social work is all
                 about, effecting change.*' (Social worker in England,
                 speaking in 2018)

Many of the social workers that I have interviewed over the years for
various projects were very clear in saying that, in practice, they did

not "*have all the answers*"; yet, they were equally clear about the need to be very thoughtful and considered when making judgements about the people they were working with at the time. As we will see later in Chapter 9, informants said how important it is to use evidence to check and to back up what may have been based on the social worker's personal feeling or 'hunch' about a family or an individual (what some have called 'practice wisdom'). However, judging people is not meant to be the same thing as being judgemental in an unhelpful way, as the following manager working in a children's service pointed out to me:

> '.......*try and look at why people are doing things and not just sort of condemn them or judge them and, you know, we do ... we do judge and it's a trick question we use in our interviews when we're interviewing social workers* [for employment in the team], *you know, what do you think about judgements and things, and they say, "Oh, we don't judge." I say, "Don't we?" That's kind of our job, though, actually. Our job is to make a judgement. So, what we're trying to make is a reasonable ... fair and legal judgement ... but if you're telling me you don't make any judgements, well, you can get out then because you're not going to be any use to me as a social worker, you just want to collect some facts for me and give me a list of things that you know.*'

Attitudes towards clients/service users and towards other professionals

What does wider research tell us about social workers' attitudes towards putting clients/service users at the centre of their practice? As we have already seen, there has been an increasing focus on getting service user/client and carer viewpoints onto the agenda for professionals ever since the early 1990s (see, for example, Beresford, 1994; CCETSW, 1997; Beresford et al, 2008; Webber and Robinson, 2012). This can also (though not always) imply working in partnership with service users wherever possible, both in practice and in educational contexts (see, for example, Beresford et al, 2007; Matka et al, 2010; Slettebø, 2013; Tanner et al, 2017).

As mentioned previously, the earlier study that I was involved in (reported in Whittington and Bell, 2001) provided research findings about what social workers and probation staff qualifying in the early 1990s thought that they had learnt or needed to learn about working in organisations and with other professionals and service users. Part of the rationale for that study was to explore the idea that joining together with others in effective inter-professional practice would be in the overall interests of users of welfare services.

A follow-up to this study, using a survey and interviews, was carried out when the three-year BA social work degree was being introduced in England (Whittington, 2003). This study involved staff in 78 Diploma in Social Work (DipSW) programmes in England, and focused on learning for collaborative practice with other professionals and agencies. The summary report provides a number of findings and recommendations, and in terms of course content, the report states that, for example:

> Interviewees were asked about materials and sources they used in helping students to work collaboratively. In summary:
> - great store was placed upon human sources, with service users the most commonly and enthusiastically cited source. (Whittington, 2003: 7, section 7.3.1)

In a more recent but small-scale Canadian-based study, Gachoud and colleagues (2012) compared social workers with nurses and medical doctors (physicians) in terms of their perceptions of what the authors call 'patient-centred practice' (PCP). Interestingly, Gachoud et al (2012: 489) merely say in a note that '[The term] "Patient" be used interchangeably with "client" since some professions are more used to one term than to the other', but the only professionals they quote using as the term 'client' are social workers. I would argue that this glosses over many issues (including power) involving the use of language by different professionals. Their study findings suggest that the physicians felt that they were the least patient-centred of the three professions they included, and the researchers say they offered two explanations: first, based on the kind of work that doctors undertook; and, second, concerning the level of accountability medicine had to the health-care system: 'it was noted that [doctors thought] professions such as nursing were more likely to be patient-centered if they are involved in daily life activities with the patient' (Gachoud et al, 2012: 488). Doctors felt that they had a sense of accountability not only to the patient, but also to the health-care system overall, while they thought that other professionals did not share this responsibility. Gachoud et al (2012: 488) suggest a 'hierarchy of patient-centredness' in which 'several nurses and a few social workers felt that their own profession was the most patient-centered, and so [they] occupied the dominant position in a hierarchy of PCP'.

To follow up on the issue of *social workers' attitudes towards other professionals*, by 2007, I had been working for some years within university-based social work programmes and we were interested in exploring what our social work students (at both BA and MA levels) thought about the inter-professional and multi-agency aspects of their practice. A colleague and I[3] had identified a fairly large-scale study by Hean and colleagues (published in 2006), which sought to research the stereotypes held by health- and social-care students about other professionals. We decided to adapt the questionnaire that these authors had developed to use with a much smaller group of our own social work students, who were following a children and families specialist pathway in their final year of study and who had completed some placement activity with other professionals.

Although our students were mainly being taught uni-professionally (unlike the cohorts in Hean et al's study), we thought that an adaptation of their questionnaire might be able to tell us in more detail about our social work students' attitudes towards various other professionals[4] (with whom they were likely to work day to day) and in terms of certain identified characteristics. As reported in our article (Bell and Allain, 2011: 271–2), we used a list of nine characteristics (based on Hean et al, 2006): academic ability; professional competence; interpersonal skills; leadership abilities; ability to work independently; ability to be a team player; ability to make decisions; practical skills; and confidence. Our results were measured quantitatively and reported showing mean scores for the whole sample (see Bell and Allain, 2011: 273–5, Tables 1 and 2) and family social workers' own scores (see Bell and Allain, 2011: 273–5, Table 3). This exercise was run with two cohorts of our students in 2007 and in 2008, first using questionnaires completed by small groups (in 2007) and in the following year by obtaining questionnaires from the class of 41 individual BA and MA social work qualifying-level students.[5]

Our results confirmed some of Hean et al's (2006) earlier results, for example, *doctors* tended to be rated highly for their 'academic ability' and for 'confidence'. Our social work students rated police highly for 'leadership abilities', but lowest among the identified professions/occupations for 'academic ability' and 'interpersonal skills'. Interestingly (also mirroring results from Hean et al) our students (characterised here as 'family social workers') rated their own profession highly on 'interpersonal skills' and the 'ability to be a team player'; however, they rated themselves much lower on 'leadership abilities' and 'confidence'. In addition to the actual results obtained, we found that the exercise allowed us to develop helpful discussions and critical reflection with our students about inter-professional and multi-agency working, as well as about the development of their own sense of professional identity/ies, which we concluded would be important professionally. The exercise also acted as a useful preparation for some larger inter-professional workshops (including midwives, early years workers and medical students) in which our social work students subsequently participated (see Villadsen et al, 2012).

A partnership-based action project

Another project that I have worked on with colleagues since 2014[6] exemplifies the importance that social workers attach to building relationships both with users of services and between professional colleagues, including those working in different sectors.[7] In the 'Mothers Apart' project, local authority social work staff developed a partnership with academic staff in the higher education sector, leading to an action research project. This is perhaps the closest that I have come to being immersed in social work practice; however, this partnership working was not always an easy or straightforward experience for the team. This project illustrates the development of a partnership that was intended to combine research with a localised support initiative (called 'Hummingbirds') for mothers whose birth children had been permanently removed from their care (by the state). Preparatory work for the pilot initiative began in a London local authority in 2013, and university staff, including myself, became involved from 2014 in order to collaboratively develop the action project (for further details of this project, see Bell et al, 2016a, 2016b; Bell, 2017: chs 3, 4 and 5 (referred to as 'project D'); Lewis-Brooke et al, 2017).

As a key part of the 'Mothers Apart' project, we all intended to make women's own voices central to the design of the practice intervention ('Hummingbirds'), and the project also reflected the overall feminist approach that we took, as explained in the following extract from one of our articles:

> Growing voices [in research and practice] suggest moral, strategic and practical imperatives to provide services that will support women in their bereavement and loss to find a new and meaningful life. Some projects in Europe are addressing the issue of parents' contributions to decision making and they aim to hear the voices of parents whose children have been removed from their care (e.g. Slettebø,

2013). This suggests that parental rights of 'access', or to contribute to decision-making about their children's future, need not necessarily be lacking when children are removed to 'out of home' care. (Lewis-Brooke et al, 2017: 8)

As part of the first stage of our 'Mothers Apart' project, we therefore interviewed ten mothers from the local area who had experienced the removal of their children; this interview material informed the subsequent development of the 'Hummingbirds' support initiative. Another extract from Lewis-Brooke et al (2017: 9) gives a flavour of the interviews that we held with these mothers, although these are interpreted mainly from the perspectives of staff[8]:

> [These interviewees] commonly expressed disbelief about what had happened to them and did not appear to understand the reasons why their children had been removed. Mothers reported rudeness from social workers or feelings of being abandoned. Women talked about having to chase the social workers to access services. They also suggested that they could not understand why services to help them were not offered, as they felt that the removal of their children had exacerbated their problems. They commonly believed that more services ought to have been offered before the decision had been made for permanent child removal.

From a feminist perspective, we noticed that women continued to firmly identify themselves as 'mothers' throughout these painful experiences of loss and grief. One of the social workers who became involved with 'Hummingbirds', and who had worked previously with an adoption service, described how in that service:

> '*What we did for a number of years was hold a Mother's Day service for the birth mothers we worked with, with a local vicar in* [the borough], *and they really, really appreciated that because they say "It's such a hard day and we're not able to rejoice and, in fact, nobody acknowledges we are mothers."*'

Lewis-Brooke et al also report that some women still hoped to have (and keep) another child, although participation in 'Hummingbirds' did seem to enable some to come to terms with having a future without children. In addition to aiming to hear the voices of mothers prior to the development of 'Hummingbirds' support (see Bell et al,

2016b), a follow-up undertaken by university-based researchers in our team involved interviewing 'Hummingbirds' staff and mothers who had participated directly in the initiative (see Bell and Herring, 2017). 'Hummingbirds' staff came from various professional backgrounds, including those with experience of working in employment or educational initiatives, as well as some qualified and experienced social workers. (The initiative itself was supported financially and with staffing by the local authority but it did not directly form part of the statutory children and families social work service.)

Feedback from the 'Hummingbirds' staff, as reported in our article (Lewis-Brooke et al, 2017: 12), suggested that:

> The team's intention is to respect and value women's ideas and encourage their ability to contribute to the ['Hummingbirds'] service offered. These women have brought painful memories and dilemmas to the group and appeared to support each other despite different life stories. Their ability to listen without judgment and without apparent jealousy to the women struggling with the pain of direct contact with their child(ren) when perhaps the woman listening has no contact with their own children, now adopted, is very humbling.

Some of the social workers who were involved with the 'Hummingbirds' initiative indicated that staff were open to sharing and learning from the users of their service (as also reported in the discussion by Slettebø [2013] of work with parents in Norway). When interviewed following their participation in 'Hummingbirds', one social worker/staff member said:

> '[Client] *has always felt cared about and well, "I really like you, I hate ...", you know, she's very, very clear how much she hates social workers and we said "Well, you know that we are social workers, don't you?" And so we have quite a laugh about that and actually to me there is a serious point underneath and I wanted to say "Social workers do care about you and it isn't this 'splitting'." But, anyway, the point for me, because I feel that I'm learning all the way through, so I'm learning from the women. Every time I meet them, I learn something new.*'

From the mothers' perspectives, the university researchers were told by some women themselves (who also declared that they 'hated' social workers) during the 'Mothers Apart' project focus group/interviews that they would prefer to define staff as 'friends' and ignore the fact that they were social workers. This seemed to be because these mothers said that they would expect help and support from friends, whereas they would have felt like acting violently towards social workers.

This project also offered the opportunity to consider *'partnership' between staff working in different sectors, and for different employers.* In the 'Mothers Apart' project, we valued taking a partnership approach as it proved important not only for funding purposes and for addressing complex project issues, but also for managing expectations. Working in a local authority–university partnership meant acknowledging our different expectations, particularly in terms of overall project outcomes; for example, university staff were expected by their employer to produce written research outputs from 'Mothers Apart', while for the local authority, the successful implementation of the pilot support initiative ('Hummingbirds') was key to the partnership's success. Goodwill on both sides was important since university staff also wanted the pilot support to be successful, while local authority staff also said that they wanted to support the research. One important way to make progress turned out to be sharing funding opportunities. The university researchers were the ones who needed to obtain ethics approval from both the university and the local authority for the research activities. They also applied for and obtained research funding for the initial and subsequent research activities (including time for interviews and payment for interview transcription), while the local authority funded the involvement of their own staff and paid for the staffing and implementation of the 'Hummingbirds' pilot initiative. One member of the team also had a foot in both camps, which was helpful!

When disseminating information about this project, we have needed to acknowledge that the outcomes are complex and that they cover both research and practice outputs. Our partnership has included being as clear as possible about whether individual team members were taking insider or outsider perspectives to either the pilot initiative or the research project, or both. On one occasion, I remember voluntarily leaving what had started out as an overall project meeting once the assembled colleagues began to discuss details of the pilot initiative, which I was hoping to evaluate in the future.[9] In addition, working as partners also involved some practitioner team members becoming research participants in so far as they were interviewed about their involvement with implementing 'Hummingbirds'. Researcher members of the team conversely attempted to maintain a neutral/

non–practitioner approach to the project (though this was not always easy). In Chapter 9, we move on to consider how social workers and others explain how they are 'knowing', 'evidencing' and 'researching' social work in various contexts.

Chapter 8 summary

There is already a great deal of discussion about relationships, partnership and collaboration between social workers, other professionals and their clients/service users. Relationship-based practice is an important development, especially in UK-based social work, which has become particularly important as a counter to managerialist tendencies in policy and practice. This chapter has discussed what social workers say about relationship work with clients/service users and with other professionals, and I have drawn upon aspects such as attitudes towards stereotyping in relation to professionals and links between partnership/collaboration and organisations, using some original research examples.

Notes

1   Howe (2008: 181) suggests that 'Social work and social care are essentially relationship-based practices even if many of the explicit techniques and statutory demands impose more formal rules of engagement. Relationships can only be conducted with skill and compassion if the worker is emotionally intelligent.'

2   Beatty further asserts that the best way for anthropologists to study emotions is by taking a detailed, narrative approach using ethnography.

3   I acknowledge my co-researcher on this project, Dr Lucille Allain, Middlesex University.

4   Our adapted questionnaire included questions about the following professions/occupations: health visitors, teachers, police, early years workers, family social workers, school nurse, Child and Adolescent Mental Health (CAMHS) staff, and doctors.

5   A comparison of results from BA and MA (family social worker) students did not show any statistically significant differences between them.

6   This is referred to as the 'Mothers Apart' project.

7   I acknowledge the partnership working of all my colleagues on this project: Sarah Lewis-Brooke, Dr Rachel Herring, Sioban O'Farrell-Pearce and Theresa So (all Middlesex University); Lynne Lehane, Karen Quinn, Nikki Bradley, Francoise Cosgrove, Jo Prosser and Brian Sharpe (all of London Borough of Tower Hamlets); and Pat Oparah (Royal London Hospital, Whitechapel). The project team would particularly like to thank

'Hummingbirds' staff and all the mothers who were interviewed and/or who were 'Hummingbirds' participants.

8   For ethics approval reasons, I am not providing direct quotes from mothers themselves in this publication.

9   In the event, university researchers were able to follow up on the results of 'Hummingbirds' with staff and participants, but a full evaluation was not feasible for various reasons.

9

Knowing and evidencing: building a research base, mapping and modelling

Introduction

As the International Federation of Social Workers (IFSW) definition makes clear, social work is considered to be *both* a 'practice-based profession and an academic discipline', and, as such, it is 'underpinned by theories of social work, social sciences, humanities and indigenous knowledge'. In Chapter 8, we examined an example project ('Mothers Apart') that combined research and a practice intervention. In this chapter, I consider policies and strategies underpinning social work research and evidence-based or evidence-informed practice, as well as considering how social workers say they generate knowledge or evidence and disseminate it to others; the dissemination of research is principally via publications such as journals, and through conferences. Later, in Chapter 10, we look at how social workers and their close academic colleagues have organised some of these kinds of knowledge- and research-based activities.

Returning to Barth's (1975: 255) anthropological work that I cited earlier, we should note his comment that the knowledge corpus that he theorised in Papua New Guinea 'will only persist to the extent that its parts are frequently re-created as messages and thereby transmitted'. This process is applicable in a tradition fully based on oral language forms, but there is a case to be made that the point about the re-creation of messages still applies in societies that are more dependent on literary/written forms of knowledge. Anyone who has ever participated in a conference (and has been involved in making last-minute amendments to their presentation) will know that there are often subtle or not-so-subtle differences between versions of their written and orally presented research; you will also appreciate what the potential impacts of these re-creation processes are for the dissemination of the work.

We have already seen that not all social workers think alike, despite affirmations that they have shared values and professional commitments;

thus, there are many relevant but different paradigms and theoretical underpinnings to social work, whether as a practice-based or an academic discipline. Subsequently, and particularly in Chapter 5, we looked in more detail at some of those different theoretical ideas, which strike the outsider as a complex guide to 'doing' social work in particular ways and different contexts; these include influential strands such as systemic, psychodynamic, relationship-based or radical approaches. Some commentators have discussed the potential for knowledge to be harnessed to advance social justice, for example, in contrast to its increasing importance for generating profit, especially in academic contexts (Heinsch and Cribb, 2018). We have already heard social workers themselves in earlier chapters of this book critiquing some of the narrower, more managerialist/proceduralist approaches to social work practice that appear to have become favoured, especially by the state in various guises and within neoliberal contexts (for example, when social workers are working with children and families [see, for example, Higgins, 2017]).

By speaking to a number of English informants for this book, have I exacerbated this critical tendency, including the idea that English social work is currently dominated by the state? I would argue that there are also neoliberal context-related, but different, issues elsewhere. For example, as we have already identified, there is a perceived lack of professional recognition (and appropriate remuneration) in some other countries in Europe (for example, in Portugal or Romania) (Weiss-Gal and Welbourne, 2008; Lazăr et al, 2019), including post-communist states in Eastern Europe (see also Pawlas-Czyz et al, 2017), as well as a changing/increasing reliance on private sector services (for example, in Denmark or Sweden). There is some ambivalence towards using evidence-based and other approaches that have been developed internationally, as the following Danish social work educator that I interviewed in 2018 explained:

> 'We have this whole idea of governance and steering of social services that is inspired from models from other countries, all the evidence programmes and the whole idea about how they can be more cost-effective from US, from Canada and places like that. Social work is very international in that sense and it has always been. I mean, look back in the history of Denmark, I think social workers were some of the, one of the professions that really travelled a lot and came home with inspiration from the UK, from Holland, from the United States and places like that. And you always see this thing about, when you see social workers come back and they're inspired

> *and they think "This is the new method" and then, at the same
> time, you also have critical voices and this kind of movement where
> you take new methods ... you're critical about.'*

This quote, suggesting that social work has always been international, open for inspiration and new methods, suggests that while being critically reflective, as this informant told me, it is also 'undogmatic'. All of these issues feed into any discussion about how research and evidence *should* provide a basis for the evaluation of welfare/social work-based services, and for wider research into social problems.

Arts or sciences, disciplinarity or interdisciplinarity? Where do social workers stand?

Our previous considerations in Chapter 5 indicated that social workers using various schools of thought may inevitably be fixed on the social and/or the psychosocial in terms of the content of their practice; yet, in terms of research and understanding, the epistemologies and contexts that social workers are working within increasingly need to include evidence from research based within the clinical or 'hard' sciences, as well as in the social sciences[1] (for the relevance of art and science to social work practice, see also Cornish, 2017). This raises some long-standing questions about boundaries between what is seen and accepted as scientific and what is not (for example, going right back to Gieryn's [1983] sociological analysis and beyond).

Looking back to the mid-1990s, commentators such as Sheppard (1998: 779) were suggesting 'a general theory of social work knowledge ... as part of a system of thought which gives as much prominence to the nature of social work as the epistemological considerations of valid knowledge'. More recently, there have been calls for social workers to be taught psychosocial studies in order to provide more coherence at a meta-theoretical level between the various elements of social work education (Frost, 2008). Partly contrasting with a social work-focused stance, other researchers suggested that interdisciplinarity should become more significant to social work (Sharland, 2012, 2013; see also the anthropologist Strathern, 2007[2]); according to some (Nurius and Kemp, 2014), interdisciplinarity can be especially important for early-stage social work doctoral researchers. From the early 2000s, interest in questions of disciplinarity and interdisciplinarity seems to have gathered pace among social workers and social work researchers, and also for bodies such as the Economic and Social Research Council (ESRC) and the Social Care Institute for Excellence (SCIE) in the UK. In 2003, for example, Ian Shaw (an academic with a background in the probation service) wrote a commentary about social work research, taking as his starting point the 2001 UK Research Assessment Exercise (RAE),[3] in which he outlined what he saw as some key questions for social work research. In addition to research quality, Shaw identifies research methodology, relationship to science, relationship between practice and research, governance and research ethics, and building research capacity as key areas for discussion. His vision for social work research is international and interdisciplinary overall, and he urges social workers and social work researchers not to be too preoccupied about whether social work is a distinct discipline.[4] However, Shaw (2003: 115, emphasis added) affirms his view that *'disciplinary issues* such as theorizing, conceptualization, doctoral level work, the practice/higher education interface and research ethics are ignored at our peril'.

A few years later, Boddy et al (2006), in response to the UK government's research governance and ethics developments (which had started in health and were being extended as a Research Governance Framework [RGF] to social care), carried out a mapping exercise of Councils with Social Services Responsibilities (CSSRs). They raised the interesting question: what counts as research in social care? While usefully focusing on issues of ethics and governance, as Shaw had earlier suggested, Boddy et al's article is noticeable, especially to an outsider, for its consistent reference to 'social care' rather than 'social work'. Was this simply meant as a more inclusive term for those who carry out social care research (the majority of whom, in these authors' description, are 'social services staff')? Is there any other reason why a profession of social work is not fully acknowledged? (Perhaps because the position of employers rather than professionals per se was being foregrounded in relation to ethics and governance requirements?)

Increasing calls in the UK for research capacity building in social work at this time, by bodies such as Joint University Council Social Work Education Committee (JUCSWEC, 2006) and the ESRC, led in 2008 to the ESRC making a call for a Strategic Adviser for Social Work and Social Care Research to guide the development of the UK research base. Elaine Sharland was appointed to this role between 2008 and 2009, producing a report in 2010 (see Sharland, 2012, 2013). As she recounts, 'the ESRC explicitly called for the Strategic Adviser to include, but not to prioritise, social work as either subject or object, in the social work and social care research frame' (Sharland, 2013: 9). Why was this? Sharland (2013: 9) herself says that she was expected to 'examine how a widely cast, loosely defined, but apparently poorly evidenced, practice and policy field, captured in one breath as "social work and social care" might be better informed by a distinctly wider, more heterogeneous and altogether more excellent disciplinary and interdisciplinary research community'. In this, she clearly faced difficulties and paradoxes. As she points out in the same article and elsewhere, '"social care" is not a recognised research discipline, nor is it a self-recognising research community' (Sharland, 2013: 9; see also Sharland, 2012). Furthermore, Sharland (2013: 10) suggests that social care, as well as social work, research was 'in need of a boost', that social work researchers 'were insufficiently developed, and that the more established cognate disciplines (with stronger research credentials[5]) do not – or not enough – engage in this field'. She thus found her brief as Strategic Adviser 'epistemologically and practically … challenging' (Sharland, 2013: 10).

Sharland (2010) suggested that social work in the UK was 'less firmly grounded than cognate disciplines in social science methodologies' and 'less grounded than health disciplines in scientific methods' (Sharland, 2013: 14). She describes how qualitative research methods were usually seen as the mainstay of social work and social care research, whereas there were identified deficits in terms of the use and knowledge of quantitative methods. (This was a point that I and my colleague tried to address when we were teaching research methods to our own social work master's students from 2006/07 [see Bell and Clancy, 2013[6]]).

Sharland (2012) gives a more detailed analysis of her work as Strategic Adviser and discusses the pros and cons of disciplinarity and interdisciplinarity for both social work and social care, concluding that while these present challenges, especially for research capacity building, 'disciplinarity and inter-disciplinarity are co-dependent. Strategies for building social work and social care research excellence and impact will best succeed if they pay heed both to distinctive disciplinary needs and to enhancing cross-fertilisation, integration and collaboration' (Sharland, 2012: 208).

Moving on to consider connections between research, evidence and practice, there are now many and increasing examples broadly relating to *evidence-based approaches* to practice within social work. Evaluation more generally, including the specific use of randomised controlled trials, may be advocated as providing good evidence (see, for example, Morago, 2006); however, they are not without methodological criticism. Furthermore, some social work-based researchers have themselves described the limitations as well as the strengths of carrying out such studies (for example, Macdonald and Turner, 2005[7]). Yet, what has been termed the 'evidence-based practice' revolution in social work/social care continues (see Soydan and Palinkas, 2014). There is continuing debate about the use of medicalised, particularly neuroscientific, and related approaches and data in divergent fields of social work (see Healy, 2016; Plafky, 2016), for example, in relation to work in mental health (for example, Sapey, 2013) or to work with parents (see Edwards et al, 2015; Garrett, 2018).

In my view, this underlines the continuing need for further exploration of what 'EBP' actually means for social workers in practice, despite the existing debates and considerable amount of published research in this area (see, for example, Avby et al, 2014; Gray et al, 2014; Scurlock-Evans and Upton, 2015); some social workers prefer the terms 'evidence-informed' or even 'research-informed' practice instead of the off-the-shelf sounding 'evidence-based practice'. Like anthropology, my feeling is that social work can also address both the social and the clinical by using diverse approaches to evidence, though the emphasis given to each in these debates continues to vary.

Building a research and evidence base: social workers' opportunities and constraints

There are two broad aspects to social workers engaging with knowing and evidencing: as noted earlier, by conducting their own research or enquiry (either as academics or practitioners); or by appreciating and acting upon published research, often under the rubric of developing evidence-based social work practice. For students, there is the third aspect of evaluating/reviewing existing research for educational purposes (see also Bell, 2017: ch 2).

Recent discussions of the opportunities and constraints that social work academics and researchers face when conducting their own research in the UK (see, for example, Moriarty et al, 2015; Teater et al, 2018) demonstrate similar findings (apparently consistent with previous research in the US). In the context of social work education, social work academics seem to experience time pressures and other constraints related to heavy teaching and administrative workloads, despite expressing enthusiasm for conducting research.

Returning to the 'Mothers Apart' project, this was constructed as a collaborative partnership between social work practitioners working in a local authority in the UK and university researchers, as well as, importantly, with input from users of social work services (see Chapter 8). An example of the application of theories into an overall model relevant to a particular area of social work practice is given in our article about this project (Lewis-Brooke et al, 2017). This model involved the development of a secure base for women, based on a combination of ideas from Schofield and Beek (2009) linked to attachment theory, Gilligan (1997) on resilience and previous work by some of the social work professionals involved with 'Hummingbirds' (Lewis-Brooke and Bradley, 2011). The 'Hummingbirds' project workers explained that 'the intervention model that was created is not a finished product, but evolved further during the pilot stage as we learnt from women who came to the ["Hummingbirds"] service' (Lewis-Brooke et al, 2017: 10). The 'Hummingbirds' model is a useful illustration of how theories, previous applications, social work practice experience and the experiences of service users could all be combined to provide a basis for a new intervention, *as well as* for associated research activities (in this case, within the wider 'Mothers Apart' project).

I had already begun in the early 2000s to take an interest in social workers' use of evidence in their practice, as well as in the more abstract theoretical schools of thought lying behind was being unproblematically called 'evidence-based practice'. A study that I participated in (Caldwell et al, 2007) involved making comparisons between recently qualified nurses, social workers, physiotherapists and occupational therapists in England, based on a survey design.[8] The project focused on: respondents' attitudes towards EBP; how confident these practitioners felt to 'engage in EBP'; and how relevant their initial training (for example, as part of their qualifying education) had been 'in relation to EBP'. (The study did not focus on the theoretical content of published research, but explored the survey respondents' uses of and access to published research.) Although I think we tended to take for granted the meaning of the term 'evidence-based practice' in this study, it was interesting to see that most of the (small number of) social worker participants reported having had education and training in the critical appraisal of research-based publications, often as part of master's-level qualifying education. Survey respondents reported on their experiences while in employment, as our article describes:

> A large majority of respondents [from all the professions surveyed] stated that they had access to electronic bibliographic databases, and that they were encouraged by their employers to read research literature relevant to their practice. However, this stands in contrast to the numbers of respondents regularly using such databases, and those who felt that their practice would improve if they had greater access to research literature. (Caldwell et al, 2007: 526)

I also began at this time to interview some social workers in more detail about their views about research, theories and EBP; I started with some who had come into academia from social work practice, and who therefore seemed to have a particular interest in research and theory. As reported in Chandler et al (2015), one of those academic informants suggested that social work theories were mostly eclectic, and this could be seen as linked to social worker identities:

> social workers don't feel very competent and very confident about their own theoretical knowledge, so they sort out theory rather than building theory, they sort it out, they've plucked it from different places, so I think it doesn't hang together necessarily well … they've tried to create this body of knowledge to make themselves feel better … to make themselves look more professional, but actually that knowledge is then disempowering even further, because nobody actually really understands it. (Chandler et al, 2015: 113)

My subsequent interviews with other English social workers and some managers working in practice (mainly in children's services) allowed me to ask them about EBP and to explore in more detail what kinds of theories they said were being used in their own social work practice; in some cases, I found out in more detail about their approaches to gathering social work evidence.[9] I have described these processes to colleagues in terms of methodologically 'wading into a sea of voices', especially at the stage of analysing the responses, but these accounts also present my own questions as interviewer and give some relevant context.

Case example A

This social worker (who I will call 'A') had been qualified for just over three years when I interviewed him in 2012 and he was working in a team that supported children with disabilities and their families. To pick up on the points made by the earlier informant about the eclectic nature of social work theory, this informant said that *"most people working in social work know that the knowledge base of social work comes from a real eclectic mix"*. When I asked him the key question of *"If I say this phrase to you, 'evidence-based practice', what do you understand by that?"*, which I was asking all informants in this project, A's response was:

'evidence-based practice I think is certainly very fashionable, and has been perhaps for the last maybe ten, maybe more, years. But then what people mean by it I think is less clear. I think perhaps a more narrow definition I understand of it would be, it would be about social research methods and using that research for evidence, maybe to the exclusion of other types of social work knowledge, which could be around practice knowledge.'

I am interested in his use of the term 'fashionable' here: is A telling me what he thinks I want to hear and also aiming to please his own managers in practice? This informant went on to articulate how he went about gathering evidence on the ground using his own observations from which to make professional judgements, linking this into theoretical issues. He seems to be following rules and yet his own uncertainties shine through; in this, he appears to be a thoughtful, intelligent social worker, as far as I am able to judge:

Interviewer: *'First of all, what does it mean for you to work, and is it possible to say what it means to work, in an evidence-based way?'*

Informant A: *'I think we make judgements, and we go in and we meet with children and families and we form hypotheses about these families. And then, clearly, we're going to have to provide some evidence of why we've come to that hypothesis. So, whether we say, "Well, I've come to this hypothesis because I've spent time with this family and I've observed x, y and z." And x, y and z could mean p, q, r or it could mean t, u, v. And whether that's "evidence-based" because I'm forming a hypothesis about a family because of what I've observed, but then am I making the right judgements? And what I think would be counted as rational thoughts, and judgements about what I'm observing, and where that's coming from. And I think there's probably another ... jumping to the evidence as well, what is the basis of me making that observation, and thinking that is the assumption? And I think that's probably the point where we should be looking at, well, what is the evidence for my conclusions rather than just the observations? And I think that then, for me, becomes a bit of a personal struggle because say, for example ... we're working with, we're working with case scenarios* [in his team and in supervision] *at the moment that*

are quite live, young … they are men with Asperger's
syndrome who are committing crimes.… [A goes on to
give some detailed theoretical background to what
he already knows and has read about this issue. He
then sums up the issue by saying the following.] So,
if practitioners can look at that evidence base there, so there
are research papers saying about the negative consequences
of going down the criminal justice route, whereas you can
also look at, well, the need to go down a criminal justice
route. So, when the social worker … people are being
hurt, and then, well, why weren't charges brought? Then
they're saying, "Well, the evidence base for that is really
unclear." … So, I think it becomes difficult in some areas.'

Interviewer: 'So, what you're suggesting I think … there may be times
when, if you like, the "evidence" itself is not clear or it's
contradictory.'

Informant A: 'Yes.'

Interviewer: 'And you're saying that's a problem, are you, for practice
based…?'

Informant A: 'I think it can be. I suppose, I also, kind of, think then
evidence is never going to be just straightforward, and it
is always going to be contested. So, what … when that
knowledge is then contested, then to say that meaningfully
you work in an evidence-based way kind of loses it a little
bit for me in terms of research, when that knowledge base
of social work is contested.'

Later in his interview, A acknowledged that in terms of overall
theoretical frameworks, he had been influenced by ideas about
attachment theory and he said that he favoured recent developments
in what he thought of as 'relationship-based practice'. It was also clear
to me that at this stage in his career, despite (or perhaps because of)
his ability to articulate his uncertainties, he wanted to tell me that he
felt supported by the team where he was working, which he described
as "a good learning environment", with regular practice meetings where
they discussed "a whole range of topics", for example, in relation to case
reviews and published research.

Case example B

At the other end of the spectrum from 'A', social work manager B,
whom I also interviewed in 2012, said that she had over 30 years

of experience in various social work roles, working for different employers, but mainly within what she termed 'child protection' (statutory) or 'child in need' services. I also asked her about evidence-based practice:

Interviewer: *'Evidence-based practice, can you say something about what you understand that phrase to mean?'*

Informant B: *'Well, I'm not sure I know what it means, if I'm being 100 per cent honest. I understand, or at least I think I understand, that it's linked to research backing up the work that we do, but it doesn't mean that to me.'*

Interviewer: *'What does it mean to you?'*

Informant B: *'For me, what it should mean is that the assessments that we carry out and the work that we do is backed up by our observations, by our understanding, by child development, by what we know from research and by all the things that make us good social workers; [we] get a feeling, the hypothesis we make as a result of that.'*

Interviewer: *'So, research is part of that but it's only one part of that?'*

Informant B: *'It's only one facet.'*

I went on to ask B what she would then understand by working in an evidence-based way:

Informant B: *'Well, I know that some of my social workers who are considerably more knowledgeable on the facet than I am would talk a lot more about research. And I see it ... when I was a chair, I saw it peppered through analysis, I saw it peppered through reports; sometimes, it felt very out of context in relation to the points people were trying to make and sometimes it felt as if people were adding it because it was expected of them.... I think, sort of, the more newly qualified workers have, obviously, that's something that is touched on.... I have to say, I mean, I qualified in 1980, it wasn't a part of what we did or even thought about so, you know.... But, we talked about other models of social work and I get the sense that evidence-based practice is part of, you know, the new way of looking at social work. And I think it has its place, don't misunderstand me, I just, I'm not 100 per cent sure that you need to know every piece of research to be a good social worker.'*

Interviewer: 'You've mentioned models and methods and things just there, so do you think there are any that have been lost maybe because of this new emphasis on being 'evidence-based'? Is there something that's been lost?'

Informant B: 'I don't know if it's been lost because of the evidence-based social work approach, but I think, you know, I trained in an era when there was more of a, I use the quote quite liberally, "therapeutic" look at social working; people talked about relationships and dependency and casework. And I sense that we've lost a lot of that in the way in which we work with families and I don't think there's very much room for it in terms of the way we work now. But I wouldn't say that we've lost models in a way, I think we've just lost a way of working.'

Later in her interview, B talks about current ways of working in social work and the connections between producing written evidence and social workers becoming deskilled:

Informant B: 'Munro talks, doesn't she, about the fact that we have, you know, we need to be spending longer with children and less time on our computers, and I think that, you know, you can't expect social workers to do any form of real social work without giving them back the freedom to do hands-on work with their children. And, you know, one of the things ... I have been absolutely staggered by the amount of stuff that we are expected to do. I, personally, think it is a complete waste of our skills. I am all for evidencing the work that we do and making sure that it's recorded appropriately, but for us to be doing that work I think is a complete ... it's the paperwork generally. I mean, you can't take anything anywhere without a raft of paperwork. For instance, we are taking a child that we have had in our care now for five years, he's been placed all that time with the same carer, we are going to panel for a view on long-term fostering for him, which I think is very appropriate. And we've just realised last week that, actually, they weren't just expecting a matching report, they were expecting the [full] placement record. I just think anyone that has looked at those records and realises how long they take to do would not be asking for that in those circumstances.'

Interviewer: *'So, would you call that "evidence"? Is that evidence that they're asking for, or what is the right word for it?'*

Informant B: *'Well, I think it's, I think, in a way, it's evidence because it's, but it's evidence linked to "their" needs as opposed to the child's needs. And I think that what happens is that we expect and, you know, and I know our senior managers are doing their best to think about this, but I think they make decisions about the way in which information is gathered and held that has huge knock-on effects for the people inputting that. And affects our ability to then do that front-line work that actually then helps you build up that relationship and the evidence that you need to make the decisions that you need to make.'*

This situation, B seems to say, then produces a dilemma for social work managers, who have become dependent on receiving evidence in the form of paperwork that has to be produced, more often than not, by front-line social workers themselves:

Interviewer: *'So, do you think that, you know, faced with all of that, do you think that individual social workers who are working with these cases, do you think that sort of ties their hands, or does that allow them some autonomy to make decisions or…?'*

Informant B: *'I think it ties people's hands because what managers measure is the paperwork; what I measure is the manager. It's something very different. Without the paperwork, I am not able to evidence, sometimes, what we do. And I don't know what the answer is because I, you know, we've lost our typing pool and all of those things, but I think we need to…. You know, people talk about "reclaiming social work", but in a way, I think that's not an exaggeration. Because, I think, whilst we expect all this to be put onto a computer and millions of forms to be completed by social workers, they're not out there doing what they should be doing.'*

Disseminating research findings and publishing from practice

I have explored knowing and evidencing in the previous section partly from the perspectives of an example practitioner and a social work manager, and we have seen how they were mainly consuming other people's research, as well as constructing evidence that is relevant for their day-to-day practice. I am aware that these are micro-examples, but their accounts do fit in with comments made by my other informants. For example, in more general terms, another English informant described to me how *"I think we're beginning to engage more with evidence-informed practice, so looking at the research evidence, evidence from evaluations and really thinking about that very deeply in terms of what difference that can make to social work practice with the people who we serve"* (transnational social worker/educator speaking in 2018). The overall picture of how social workers connect with research findings and use these in practice is sure to be very complex and will also be expected to vary depending on the national policy context, as the following recently interviewed European informant described to me. In her view:

> *'Social workers should engage with new technologies and then ... you know, [if they want] some kind of professional identity and competent forms of discretion, then they have to know more about research. They have to know more about big data, they have to know more about how things are quantified and registered, and how this is used for governance and for prioritising social services and for packaging services for people with different characteristics. It's kind of, it's also standardising trends in the way that services are delivered.... So, if you have to have, professionals should be able to, kind of, not only be, you could say, automatically following the packages or the decisions that the systems and the technologies suggest ... they have to be really strong in terms of what, how they view this individual person's problems, or does it actually fit with this output ... that you can get from data.'* (See also Shore and Wright, 2015)

My explorations into *journal publishing*,[10] as both a participant and, on occasions, as a journal reviewer, reveal a diverse world of ever-increasing publishing opportunities for social workers and researchers to place research data, in both closed and, increasingly, open-access forms. The previous discussions of disciplinarity and interdisciplinarity should indicate that it is not straightforward to decide (especially internationally) exactly which journals and the data they contain are relevant to social workers, or to social work as an academic discipline. In terms of assessing research quality, there are currently (as of 2019) 42 journals listed in the social work area of the Thomson Reuters

Incites Journal Citation Reports, which is a recognised source of journal impact factors and other information. However, we should also note that this influential database has been criticised by some social work researchers/academics (Blyth et al, 2010[11]) for its coverage, relevance to social work as a discipline and reliance on metrics to assess quality.

I will not spend very long on processes of peer review for journals except to say that while I am sure that colleagues from all disciplines take this responsible task seriously, it is inevitably somewhat subjective, and this is almost bound to lead to injustices for individual researchers on occasion. Who has not had the experience of sending a paper to a journal, being asked for specific revisions (which are carried out), only to then be told 'No, that isn't what was required.' You are left asking: (why/how) did I get it wrong? As a reviewer, I have sometimes found it easier to dismiss an article that seems obviously out of place for that particular journal than to suggest improvements for a paper that still feels somehow unsettling but appears to fit. Has my subjective bias somehow crept in, and, if so, how? Questions of disciplinarity are thus often important. Reviewing can be a lonely process, and it is sometimes an immense relief to read (post-reviewing) someone else's review of the same article, where the other reviewer has obviously had the same thoughts. Like social workers who are in practice, I am sure that all researchers acting as journal reviewers sometimes doubt the relevance of their own subjectivity: what evidence have we brought to bear? What if we had made an unfair judgement about something that may be of crucial relevance to another person's career?

In terms of *conferences*, it is encouraging to see more connections being made in recent years between organisations that sponsor journals, conferences and other research or evaluative activities, including universities, especially internationally (for example, the European Social Work Research Association and the European Association of Schools of Social Work, which both sponsor conferences). At national levels too, there have been important developments: in the UK, the Joint University Council, Social Work Education Committee runs an annual (JSWEC) conference and supports the journal *Social Work Education*; and in Europe, developments include annual Social Work International Conferences held at the University of Bucharest, Romania, since 2016, and celebrations of a decade of social work education and research at the Instituto Universitário de Lisboa (ISCTE), Portugal, held in 2018. In Chapter 10, we move on to considering how some of these and other social work activities have been organised in the period since 1990.

Chapter 9 summary

Professional and occupational groups may be expected to develop their own knowledge base(s) that will often be situated within specific epistemological frameworks, though the nature of such frameworks is often contested. In this chapter, we have explored how, within social work and social care, theoretical models and methods of gathering evidence from practice are explained and used. Social work, though emphasising the social, may be expected to draw upon an eclectic range of social and clinical sciences, with issues of disciplinarity and interdisciplinarity being identified as an important aspect of how knowledge of different kinds, although contested, can be applied to social work practice and research. I have begun to indicate the development of social work-related organisations concerned with knowledge in different places, and will explore these activities in more detail in Chapter 10. I have given examples in this chapter from my own research of how social workers have explained what evidence looks like to them and how they have attempted to work with evidence and research in their practice.

Notes

[1] As mentioned previously, Holland (1999) gives us a useful meta-theoretical view of differing possibilities, and suggests the significance of reflexivity in managing our understanding of all these perspectives.

[2] Some interesting recent work linking social work with anthropology, influenced by anthropologists Marilyn Strathern, Martin Holbraad and Morten Pedersen, includes the Matrix Research Project at the University of Luxembourg, organised by Claude Haas and Thomas Marthaler.

[3] Records show that the 2001 RAE aimed to 'enable the [UK] higher education funding bodies to distribute public funds for research selectively on the basis of quality. Institutions conducting the best research receive a larger proportion of the available grant.' Using a standard scale, various panels of assessors provided 'quality ratings for research across all disciplines' (Research Assessment Exercise, 2001).

[4] Prior to Shaw's commentary, Lyons and Orme (1998) had published a survey analysis of social work input to the 1996 RAE with its social work and social policy panel. Out of 42 academic departments responding to this survey, 17 submitted to the RAE as 'social work only', 15 as part of wider groupings (for example, with social policy or else with sociology, nursing, education and so on), while in ten departments, social work was not included in RAE submissions (for example, due to having few research-

active staff), though some respondents were reportedly disappointed by their institution's decision in this respect.

[5] Presumably, psychology, sociology and social policy in particular.

[6] This article and that by Sharland (2013) were published in a journal special issue reflecting contributions to five methodology conferences held under the ESRC Research Development Initiative (RDI) 14 during 2010–11, which had aimed 'to enhance the research skills and attitudes towards research of mid-career social work academics in the UK' (McDonald, 2013: 3).

[7] This project is further discussed in Bell (2017) as 'Project A'.

[8] This project is further discussed in Bell (2017: ch 6) as 'Project P'.

[9] The following complex case examples are meant to illustrate how an anthropologist asks someone in detail about what they do and what they say they do to provide a quasi-ethnographic picture (see, again, Hockey, 2002, 2014; see also Gordon and Cooper, 2010).

[10] This could also include social workers' increasing involvement with social media, blogs and so on, as well as other informal means of disseminating research and professional information. My main focus here has been on formal publications, but see, for example, Megele and Buzzi (eds) (2020).

[11] These authors proposed 'an alternate fair, inclusive and transparent system for assessing the quality of publications based on peer evaluation and incorporating an ethical approach consistent with the discipline's professional values' (Blyth et al, 2010: 120).

Organising: influences of the state, organisations and wider social policies

Introduction

Organising social work falls into many different areas, and because social workers are employed in so many different kinds of organisation (statutory local authorities being only one kind) and different sectors (including health and education, as well as the social-care field), trying to analyse such forms of organisation directly in terms of employing organisations would be a mammoth task. A more fruitful approach seems to be to concentrate on a few areas, which will allow us to look backwards and forwards across our time frame of the 1990s to the present day, as well as on into the future, and also to consider social work both internationally and in the UK.

We have already considered some important areas of social work in previous chapters, so those I have chosen to examine here continue these themes: the development of professional organisation(s), research conferences (continuing from Chapter 9) and the further exploration of developments in social work/social care education. In the final sections of this chapter, I will give two specific English examples: the first links up social work/social care training, research and related workshops and conferences in the 1990s, in which I was involved; and the second explores how recent social work education has been organised via the UK government initiative of funded 'Teaching partnerships'.

Professional organisation(s)

As we first noted in Chapter 2, debate continues internationally about the significance of social workers being agents of the state, and many of the social workers that I have interviewed imply that 'real' social work (whether in its caring or controlling aspects) is mainly about their relationships with those whom they serve. However, in Chapter 8, we also noted the view that social workers need to be able to make judgements about complex social and personal situations; from this viewpoint, they cannot act alone or merely consider themselves to be non-judgemental, but should be prepared to act responsibly, legally and in accordance with supervision from senior colleagues in order to achieve their goals. Chapter 7 also explored what can happen when social workers' fitness to practise is questioned in the context of supervision and worker management.

The ways in which their profession is organised and recognised is thus important to social workers across Europe. Social work education is also an important factor. Furthermore, social workers' underlying values (which we explored in Chapter 7) include acting in the public interest, with the implication that they should fit in with the aims of organisations that employ social workers, as well as with policies developed at the state level. This fitting in applies as much to social work education and its underlying policies as to direct social work practice with users of services. This places social workers in an ambivalent position, as already noted by an English informant that I quoted at the beginning of Chapter 7.

In Chapter 3, we saw that in the UK, The College of Social Work (TCSW) (which had been established in 2012 as a subscription-based organisation) collapsed in 2015 following the withdrawal of government financial support; debates have continued about the causes and implications of its demise, with sections of the UK press describing this as 'a tragic end to a promising project' (McNicoll, 2016; see also Brindle, 2015). The collapse seems to have come about as much from social workers not subscribing to the organisation, resulting in financial problems, as being due to any perceived vindictiveness by the state. My English and transnational informants who discussed TCSW in their interviews were somewhat split over these events: some were disappointed, having seen TCSW as a real chance for developing an independent professional organisation; others recognised the usefulness of some of TCSW's outputs (particularly the Professional Capabilities Framework) but preferred to move on by backing the existing professional organisation (the British Association of Social Workers [BASW]) and the associated Social Workers Union, recently established as an organisational member of BASW. According to the BASW website, the Social Workers Union is involved in active campaigns and supported a recent study and report (Ravalier, 2018) on UK social workers' working conditions and well-being by an academic psychologist, which was discussed in the House of Lords in 2018.

Elsewhere in Europe, I have been aware of professional organisations for social workers becoming established, for example, in Romania, where the National College of Social Work was established in 2005, as we saw in Chapter 3. The following informant described how one current professional challenge was to ensure the professional recognition of social workers:

> '*The first step is to have more and more people qualified and ... [not] employing people from other professions, with other qualifications or with no qualifications. We even have high-school graduates working in some rural areas. It's not uncommon to see this situation or law or administration graduates who are there and, obviously, they do unattractive work.... Now there are some initiatives in this respect, even the Ministry for Labour has some projects and some strategies. For instance, now they have a programme by which they plan to have in 1,000 municipalities ... in about one third of them, they will finance the establishment of social work services and they will pay a salary for one social worker. So, this is changing, we know this, and this is progress which was a long time fought for.*' (Social worker/educator speaking in 2018)

There is a similar story in Portugal, where the organisation of professionals is reportedly affected by labour market deregulation:

> '*There are other dimensions of the social worker role that can be developed, that can be practised beyond the cash benefits. For instance, in Portugal, one big thing that we have also in professional life is the complete deregulation of the labour market for social workers. Although we have the title of "social worker", it's protected by law, it is defined by law, who can be entitled as social worker, but even so, in actual functioning of the labour market, what we see is lots of other professionals coming to the field of social work, lots of public announcements saying, "We want to hire a social worker and his or her background can be social work or sociology" ... which is not a legal thing, but it actually happens. Even when the professional space of the social worker is respected, also what we see is a very strong tendency to hire social workers at a very low wage, which is another form of deregulating the market.*' (Social worker/educator speaking in 2018)

Social work conferences: taking up international and interdisciplinary perspectives

An area of organisation where social work professionals and academics can have some opportunities to present new developments, including critical perspectives, is during professional conferences. As we started to consider in Chapter 9, conferences and journals are, as might be expected, key means of disseminating research and also evidence that has been generated from practice; as we also saw in Chapter 9, there are continuing issues about how the disciplinary and interdisciplinary aspects of social work and social care are defined and presented, for example, through these dissemination activities. So, in this section, I want to take up these issues in relation to one particular series of international conferences; this also allows us to examine the wider issue of social networks, which is important for social workers and academics who are developing and maintaining such activities.

In 2011, an inaugural conference entitled 'Social Work and Social Care Research: Innovation, Interdisciplinarity and Impact' was held in Oxford, UK. The conference planning committee, chaired by Ian Shaw, included social work academics such as Elaine Sharland and colleagues from different parts of the UK and Australia. Interestingly, they were joined by the director of the National Institute for Health Research (NIHR) School for Social Care Research, who stated on the conference website that:

> We are pleased to be involved in the first of the European Social Work Research conferences, particularly because the wider social care perspective will be represented in the programme and hopefully in the interests of participants. In the School we are working hard to encourage and develop interdisciplinary learning and multidisciplinary collaboration in our research on adult social care practice.

This first European social work research conference included more than 160 conference contributions from different countries, including 36 from England, and smaller clusters from Belgium (seven), Finland (seven) and Sweden (nine), with a few others from a range of countries, such as Austria, Bulgaria, Canada, China, Denmark, Greece (Cyprus), Israel, Japan, the Netherlands, Portugal, Romania, Slovenia and the US. The keynote speakers at this initial conference were Professor Eileen Munro (UK), Professor Joan Orme (UK), Professor Marketta

Rajavaara (Finland), Professor Bruce Thyer (US) and Professor Peter Sommerfeld (Switzerland).

The following year (in 2012), a second conference, focused on 'Social Work Research in Local, National and International Contexts: The Challenges of Comparison and Generalisation', was held in Basel, Switzerland. This time, the five keynote speakers were: Sue White (UK), who spoke about 'designing humane European social work services'; Andreas Walter (Germany), whose talk focused on 'support across the life course' and who presented 'a comparative model of how social problems, needs and rights are constructed'; Jeanne Marsh and Daniel Gredig (US and Switzerland, respectively), who compared research, development and innovation in social work practice in the US and Europe; and Darja Zaviršek (Slovenia), who considered international perspectives on the 'academisation of social work' through doctoral studies. This time, there were slightly fewer conference contributions coming specifically from England, but many more contributors reporting on internationally focused projects; noticeably, some of these contributions focused on research methodologies. In terms of different contributors, there were still clusters of individuals from Belgium, Finland and Sweden, now joined by some from Germany, Greece (Cyprus), Israel, the Netherlands, Portugal, Switzerland and the US; individual contributors also attended from Australia, Austria, Canada, China, Denmark, Luxembourg, Mozambique, Norway, Spain, Slovenia and the US.

By 2013, when the conference was held in Jyvaskyla, Finland, it remained international but we also began to see the influence of conference location, with three of the five keynote speakers coming from Nordic countries (Teppo Kröger and Tarja Pösö from Finland, and Björn Blom from Sweden); the other keynote speakers were Adrienne Chambon (Canada) and Frank Wang (Taiwan). Conference contributors included around 30 from Finland (oral and poster presentations), with a similar number from the UK and smaller clusters from Belgium, China, Denmark, Germany, Ireland, Israel, Italy, Lithuania, the Netherlands, Norway, Slovenia, Sweden and the US.

The fourth European conference (in 2014) was held in Bolzano in Italy and was entitled 'Private Troubles or Public Issues? Challenges for Social Work Research'. Keynote speakers here included Walter Lorenz, Edward Mullen, Ian Shaw and Idit Weiss-Gal. To give a flavour of the invited contributions, potential delegates were this time asked to send abstracts relating to any of the following themes:

• Knowledge production and public accountability in social work.

- Research in social work as a participative learning process.
- Standing up to complexity – specific and universal issues in social work.
- Evidence and uncertainty – pathways to accountable social work research and practice.
- Social diversity: promoting human rights and the role of research.
- Social work and political action: what has research to do with this?

Once again, delegates came from many countries, including a large number from Italy, as well as some from Belgium, Bosnia/Herzegovina, the Czech Republic, Denmark, England, Estonia, Finland, Germany, Greece, Japan, Latvia, Lithuania, the Netherlands, Norway, Portugal, Romania, Russia, Slovenia, Spain, New Zealand, Puerto Rico, Scotland, Switzerland, Sweden, Turkey, the US and Wales.

By now, it was clear that the original conference was expanding through 'Europe and beyond', as the conference booklet for 2015 declared. This fifth conference ('Re-visioning Social Work with Individuals, Collectives and Communities: Social Work Research') was held in Ljubljana, Slovenia, with an international review panel representing 22 countries, some of whom are familiar names from their involvement in previous conferences. The organisers stated that this conference was now 'the annual showcase event of the newly established European Social Work Research Association (ESWRA)'. As the conference booklet that year explained:

> our conference call was answered by 677 abstracts authored by one or more persons. The review panel accepted 468 researchers who will present their work either orally or as poster presentations. A majority of presenters come from Western countries of the EU [European Union]: 391 in total. Sixty-five presenters come from one of the post-socialist countries, and 78 from outside Europe. Greece, Cyprus, Serbia, Georgia, Lithuania, Ukraine and Kazakhstan are the countries who have one representative each ... assembled here are researchers in social work from no less than 42 countries of the world.

The organisers of the sixth conference in Lisbon, Portugal, in 2016 ('Reflective Social Work Practices in Contemporary Societies: Dialogues and New Pathways between Praxis and Research') similarly gave information about conference participants, organisers and ESWRA Special Interest Groups in the conference booklet:

Our conference call was answered by around 700 abstracts authored by one or more persons. The review panel was integrated by 105 experts in Social Work research, from 26 different nationalities. Each abstract submitted had at least a double peer-blinded review. Moreover, almost all submissions were reviewed by peers from different nationalities and from other countries than the ones of the proposals. This complex and exigent process gives us ... the high scientific standard of the 250 oral presentations, 31 symposia & workshops and 25 posters accepted. The Conference will have 525 participants from 41 countries across Europe and other regions of the world: a majority come from European Union countries (80% of the participants, including 40 participants from Portugal and other countries of Southern Europe), but also from North America (39 researchers from United States and Canada), the Middle East and Asia (46 researchers), and Australia, which represents the highest number of researchers involved in ESWRA conferences and, for the first time, the conference programme formally includes pre-conference activities promoted for some ESWRA Special Interest Groups.

Since 2016, large, successful and international ESWRA conferences have been held in Aalborg, Denmark (seventh, in 2017) and Edinburgh, Scotland (eighth, in 2018), with annual membership of ESWRA now offered to those who attend as part of the conference fee. The forthcoming ninth conference this year (2019), to be held in Leuven, Belgium, is focused on 'the ways social work research and practice can operate in context of changing welfare state paradigms, and ... how core values of human rights and social justice can be embodied and realised' (ESWRA 2019, 2019).

This review of the development of what is now the ESWRA annual conference is intended to show both how social work is international (as claimed by almost all of the informants that I interviewed in 2018) and that this global approach is possible here precisely because we are seeing social work as an interdisciplinary academic discipline, into which its various practice-based and contingent manifestations based in localised/national settings feed (as discussed in Chapter 3). Individual key players are also visible in this review, with network links, for example, to those who are involved in social work and social work research both internationally and at national policy levels.

My own participation at many of these ESWRA conferences as a presenter means that, as mentioned earlier, I feel that I have been shifting my identity towards becoming more of a social work researcher who feels at home in this interdisciplinary and international atmosphere. However, the large number of presentations and broad streams in each conference would also allow those who identify more closely as social work practitioners or users of social work to participate on their own terms. National and international, and disciplinary and interdisciplinary, boundaries could therefore, it is hoped, be successfully crossed. However, it may be that those who are more explicitly focused on the practical aspects of social work, rather than on social work as an academic discipline per se (including some of my key informants for this book), would be less likely to attend this particular conference. Other international conferences may also appeal more to those involved in areas such as social work education (for example, the European Conference of Schools of Social Work), which, in 2019, is focused on challenging the concept of quality in neoliberal contexts.

At national and regional levels, many conferences and workshops, often on a much smaller scale, are vehicles for social work practitioners, educators and users of social work services to come together to share experiences. These kinds of events often combine policy, organisational and research issues, as in my next example, which goes back to the early/mid-1990s.

Looking back to the 1990s: organising and researching education and workforce training for Community Care skills and knowledge

As already discussed in Chapter 4, in the mid-1990s, I had begun to get involved in educational policy work, mainly to do with Community Care policy changes, at the Central Council for Education and Training in Social Work (CCETSW), London and South-East England region. By 1994/95, CCETSW wanted to find out how the wider workforce in their region was being prepared to work in the context of Community Care. I was asked to participate in a wider review of Community Care training with CCETSW staff and a consultant who was knowledgeable about this field (see Bell et al, 1997).[1] We should note that 'workforce training' could include all kinds of staff, including qualified professionals employed as social workers, as well as unqualified care workers and middle or senior managers. All these people would need to understand and work with the Community Care ethos and policies. A survey of relevant respondents was therefore proposed, to include questionnaires and telephone interviews in the first stage, with a second stage comprising more detailed interviews carried out by the consultant.

To be consistent with the prevailing Community Care policy discourse, we decided to split our survey into separate parts aimed at the purchasers and providers of training. We therefore designed two separate questionnaires with slightly different questions: first, an (orange) questionnaire for the purchasers of training, which included employers in local authorities (the statutory sector, that is, social services departments) or in the voluntary or private sectors providing Community Care-based services; and a (blue) questionnaire intended for the larger number of training providers, which included these same employers, offering training at various levels outside the Diploma in Social Work (DipSW) and/or sponsoring social work students taking the DipSW, as well as educational institutions offering the DipSW itself. I gradually came to realise that organisations themselves, and staff within them, might be designated as providers (of training *or* of services) or as purchasers; those staff who were purchasing services were generally known as 'care managers', which, as we will see, raised further issues for education and training. As we noted in our report (Bell et al, 1997: 5), it was relatively easy to identify a survey sample of representatives from statutory agencies in the region but more problematic to ensure appropriate coverage of 'the full range of organisations involved in community care'.

A framework of common topics (now termed 'competency areas') was devised as the basis for suitable questions on both questionnaires, covering: the philosophical basis of community care; assessment and care planning; inter-professional and inter-agency working; business skills; and management and organisational issues. Questions concerned the representative's own role, the kinds of training purchased or provided (within the competency areas), and the intended recipients of the various kinds of training. We also asked everyone an open-ended question about their views on the 'adequacy of existing qualifications'.

As noted in our report (Bell et al, 1997), in the first stage of the project, we received questionnaires from, and interviewed by telephone:

- 52 *training providers*, including institutional representatives of 16 DipSW programmes and 22 London boroughs or county authorities, and 14 representatives from the voluntary, private and health sectors (including what were termed 'training agencies and assessment centres'); and

- 30 *training purchasers*, including 19 from London boroughs or county authorities, and 11 from the voluntary, private and health sectors.

Apart from academics/social work educators working on DipSW programmes, the individuals that we interviewed were typically designated as 'training managers' (see also Bell, 2007a) whose job was to arrange, purchase or provide workforce training within their organisations for staff from various backgrounds working in local authorities or in the voluntary or private sectors, including sponsorship for individuals to undertake the DipSW in a college or university. I remember being completely focused on the logic of this (*Symbolic?*) purchaser–provider split, even though some organisations that we surveyed were placed in both categories (we interviewed 12 individual representatives about both functions, the rest according to whether they were designated as 'purchasers' or 'providers').

Looking back, results from this review are illuminating in terms of how preparations for the implementation of Community Care were being constructed at the time by all parties and, using the metaphor from my previous work for the CCETSW-King's College (C-K) project, the kinds of flexible scripts with which the survey respondents were working (see, again, Chapter 4). It was evident from our survey data that there were obvious perceived time lags between the introduction of Community Care policies and the impact of the new DipSW programmes, and that survey respondents' views about the training needs of their staff were sometimes pessimistic in this respect. These views sometimes focused on specific aspects of training. For example, when asked 'Are the existing qualifications available to your staff sufficient to equip them to work competently in Community Care?', the following respondent said: "*People who qualified* [in social work] *some time ago are not qualified to work competently in Community Care because their training did not include the 'needs-led' perspective, nor the business orientation.*" It was sometimes perceived that qualified social work staff therefore needed more training in skills such as contracting, negotiating and care management. For others, the main concern was with their unqualified staff, as the following respondents pointed out: "*DipSW is fine. Post-qualifying and advanced awards seem to be adaptable and therefore adequate*"; and "*We remain with a very high ratio of unqualified staff. Very often, these are the people who have the highest client contact, hence our move towards NVQs* [National Vocational Qualifications]."

In Stage 2 of this survey project, further in-depth interviews with organisational representatives were done by our consultant, and these elicited more interesting material, present in our project report (Bell et al, 1997). For example, as the pace of change in implementing Community Care policies quickened (by 1995/96), some interviewees were still reporting uncertainty about the evolution of language, as well as the direction of travel: 'It seems to change from week to week. It feels as if we're a ship ploughing through the waves – they keep coming at us, and sometimes we don't know which direction we're supposed to be going in' (Bell et al, 1997: 8). There was also some evidence from these interviews that while we had placed an overall emphasis on the division between purchasers and providers, this distinction had much less meaning for some of our interviewees (see also Freeman, 2017).[2]

Postscript: participating in a national conference and CCETSW workshops

As a postscript to all this survey work, I participated in a national two-day conference (in March 1994)[3] sponsored by CCETSW, at which our preliminary survey results were presented, as well as in two workshops (in March 1995 and February 1996) run by CCETSW London and South-East England region. These also followed up on both stages of our survey project, and offered opportunities to share information and issues about training for work in Community Care.

At the conference event, there were a number of key speakers who I knew were all 'movers and shakers' in the field of Community Care at that time. Key themes for day one of the conference, involving the key speakers, were listed on the agenda as 'Challenges for social work education' followed by 'Business culture', 'User involvement' and 'Collaboration'. On the second day, workshops were also held covering 'Purchasing and contracting', 'User trainers', 'Networking' and 'Equity and advocacy'.

Around 40 participants attended the conference, some representing local authority-based trainers, but most were 'providers' from university or college courses, with a few people described as 'independent consultants', including myself. Prior to the conference, we had all been allocated to a specific working group (these were to meet up three times during the conference). Our main group tasks were to:

- 'Identify the TYPES OF CHANGES to professional social work which are likely to be associated with Community Care now and in the future'; and
- 'Compare the "HOPES/GAINS" associated with these changes with the "DIFFICULTIES/LOSSES".'

We were also asked to produce a working agenda and to present ideas/issues/resolutions that our group wished to feed back to the whole conference.

Notes that I made on the day suggested that in addition to the overall topics being discussed, some of the speakers were keen to hasten the pace of change towards (variously): the adoption of more business-like models of social care practice; encouraging social workers to work more effectively with health (especially at the level of primary care); and breaking down boundaries between different levels of health care (for example, primary and secondary care). Above all, barriers to collaboration of all kinds needed to be broken down. Some of the 'threats' to collaboration that the speakers and group participants identified were:

- social workers and social services departments were still in provider mode (that is, their priorities still involved providing services);
- there was hostility to the Community Care reforms, as well as an absence of vision;
- management cultures within social services departments were defensive;
- social workers lacked skills for undertaking holistic assessment, it being suggested that no one knows how to do needs-led assessments;
- social work values did not include taking financial responsibility (that is, dealing with budgets); and
- there were fears about deskilling and of other professionals 'stealing a march' on social workers (for example, those working in mental health might attempt to move into social work roles).

Challenges for social work education were said to include: needing to place greater emphasis on user and carer perspectives; obtaining suitable student placements; addressing outcomes; and working with other professional cultures. In contrast to a rather negative picture overall, opportunities for social workers could be grasped (it was said) by working more collaboratively with primary health–care teams.

At the two follow–up CCETSW workshops held in 1995 and 1996 (by which time I was mainly working for an academic institution), participants identified various issues connected to the organisation and distribution of funding (particularly between agencies) as a key issue, though not a lack of financial resources per se. Workshop notes show, for example, that a statutory sector participant (from social services) commented that in terms of training "*the bulk of the energy and resources are going to care management*" (that is, to purchasing staff, rather than staff who were defined as providers of services). For voluntary sector workshop participants, there seemed to be greater emphasis on training for users of services, especially in advocacy skills. Discussion by participants about different models for Community Care training in 1996 suggested that trying to offer jointly funded, inter-agency training sometimes presented complex difficulties, especially where staff from large numbers of different agencies were involved; this, it was said, could be offset by working with designated training sections.

This extended case example has been intended to show in detail how those of us who were involved in helping to construct and implement social work educational policy in England in the early to mid-1990s specifically addressed the legislation and evolving policies around Community Care. As well as reviewing and evaluating the impacts on social work education and training, an important aspect of this work was clearly to disseminate and control key messages from the regulator (as a representative of the state), in partnership with other experts, to appropriate audiences, particularly at conferences and workshops. I noted that the majority of attendees at the national 'Revolution' conference, for example, came from university and college DipSW programmes.

Freeman (2017: 196) argues that policy (and policymaking) is a 'communicative practice' that is 'uncertain and contingent, and about promoting, halting and reversing change'. He also argues that, in itself, policy is a 'kind of caring'. As a participant observer at this time, I was very much 'in the moment', so I inevitably supported the overall direction of these policy changes and presentations, although I was also aware of voices of dissent. This concerned not only the difficulties of implementing some of the changes on the ground, but also the underlying discourses that seemed to favour a "*business orientation*", as one of the respondents I have quoted pointed out. With hindsight, one key area that also came to the fore at this period (and that my more recent interviewees have spoken positively about) was in placing greater emphasis on the empowerment of those in receipt of social work services[4] (albeit while they were also being re-categorised as 'consumers'). I would therefore have to concur with Freeman that when becoming involved in social work educational policy in the early 1990s, we did genuinely care about what we were attempting to do as in the best interests of both service users and professionals.

Looking ahead to social work education in the 21st century: the example of teaching partnerships in England

In this final section, I want to explore some of my key informants' views and experiences of a much more recent example of policy and practice in social work education: Social Work Teaching Partnerships. Following the Croisdale-Appleby and Narey Reports (both produced in 2014), the UK government decided to establish funded partnerships in England from 2015 onwards. The report of an evaluation carried out on four pilot teaching partnerships was produced in 2016 (see Berry-Lound et al, 2016). This report explains that key drivers for the UK government in setting up the scheme were to: 'enhance partnership arrangements between Higher Education Institutions (HEIs) and employers; attract more able students; embed the knowledge and skills into academic curricula and Continuing Professional Development (CPD) for existing workers; and overall raise the quality of social work practice' (Berry-Lound et al, 2016: 6).

From 2016, the scheme was extended to other regional areas, and successful applications were then funded for a certain period between 2016 and 2018/19 (for some successful partnerships, their funding was further extended within this time period). A key part of this scheme was to apparently put employers 'in the driving seat' within partnerships, and the applications that were made for funding, though produced collectively, had an employing organisation as lead applicant. I do not intend to present a full discussion of this scheme here for reasons of space (for a fuller assessment, see, for example, the initial evaluation report and its recommendations [Berry-Lound et al, 2016]); however, I will draw upon comments from some recent informants that I interviewed in 2018, all of whom were very experienced social workers involved in three separate social work teaching partnerships within England.[5] These included partnerships involving one or more HEIs, local authorities and some voluntary or third sector organisations.

As part of these recent interviews with English social work informants, we discussed current and future developments in social work education, and they were able to shed light on what being involved with teaching partnership schemes had entailed. All the people that I interviewed could see positive elements to the initiative. For example, the following social worker/educator employed in a university could see the potential for links with the HEI and impacts on future workforce development:

'The benefit of the teaching partnership is that the employer understands a lot more [about] the student journey and the importance of the placement as a learning opportunity for students, and if the employer impresses there, and values learning within teams etc, then they've got a much better likelihood of getting the brightest and the best of our students to work with them afterwards. And that's when the transformational aspect can occur within those organisations, in terms of getting good bright people in to work with families etc, in their area. So, there are a lot of benefits.'

When I asked about employers taking the lead in teaching partnerships, this next informant gave a positive yet realistic response:

'I don't see our teaching partnership in the sense of pushing social work education back to the employer. I think my experience within our partnership has been, it has been more proactive with employers about what they're looking for, rather than pushing it back to them in that sense, because I think they don't want it.... At the bottom, they don't, they've got enough going on with, you know, all the other things we've been talking about, rather than wanting to take on educating students as well. So, I think it's been more, you know, what are your agendas, what are your priorities, what are our priorities, how do we sort of join them?'

This same informant also indicated that a priority for HEIs within teaching partnerships would be to say to employers: "*We absolutely need you to give placements now for the students, we need good statutory placements.*"

Another informant could see the benefits of working in her partnership but she also touched on the issue of heavy workloads that was implied in the earlier pilot evaluation (see Berry-Lound et al, 2016):

'I think the teaching partnership, based in the university, does have an advantage because it's working with existing local authorities and trying to foster relationships and partnerships beyond what was there before, but it's not making it up, it's not inventing something new; it's building up what was there. So, I think it's a really good model. It's been frustrating because it's been so exhausting, and I think there aren't enough people around to do the work, and to manage it, but it's very meaningful for me.'

This next informant also concurred that it was important to build on existing links: "*Prior to the teaching partnership, we* [in the HEI] *had very good working relationships with those local authorities. So, the teaching partnership hasn't changed that relationship, you know, in an unrecognisable way; it was always there.*" This informant also suggested that there could be positive effects from the teaching partnership in terms of the involvement of service users and carers:

> '*We have really pushed for our service user and carer colleagues to take front and centre stage in the teaching partnership and whilst our university has always done that, it is the case the other partner university hasn't, and the local authorities are a bit behind the times in really valuing what it is that service users and carers offer. So, I think, strategically, it's been a very important vehicle.*'

As well as these positive aspects, there were some aspects of the organisation of teaching partnerships that my informants found challenging:

> '*I think where there are tensions with* [our teaching partnership] *sometimes is the lead partner decides, well, this should happen and tells the others, "This is what we're going to do." Then, you know, other people say "What authority have you got … to tell us what to do, you know, where did that come from?" So, I think there is, you know, you've got to sort of hold that* [leadership] *lightly really haven't you?*'

Another informant working with a different teaching partnership had a similar experience, which took time to resolve through negotiation and through the recognition of cultural differences between the different organisations involved:

> '*I think one of the bad things about the teaching partnership was there was an assumption made by employers that they could say what they wanted and the universities would then have to deliver it. And that's not what a partnership is about, that's a really poor understanding of this notion of partnership. So, when you think about how groups work, you know you have the "forming, storming, norming and performing", and I think we were in the "storming" stage for quite a while. But we've kind of gotten over that and there was a lot of work done in the first year of that teaching partnership, and it felt like in the second year, we've really*

achieved a lot because of all of that hard work that was done in the first year.'

It was clear that many of the achievements from teaching partnerships that my informants referred to involved developments that all parties would like to see continued into the future. These activities, including placement provision and the introduction of social work practitioners into HEIs as part-time teachers, would be expected to enhance links between employers and HEIs, and to contribute positively to social work education and workforce development (see also Hingley-Jones et al, 2019). However, the teaching partnership scheme, involving significant UK government funding, has also been time-limited, and informants did not necessarily see continuing this initiative as a future government priority. Some informants were therefore concerned about how to maintain some of these positive developments on a sustainable basis:

> '*We've had a lot of money given to us to, in a way, push ahead with these developments and there's an expectation that this pump-priming will then lead to changes being made in local authorities, so that things can continue as business as usual after the teaching partnership money goes. Well it ain't like that because alongside of this money, local authorities are still facing cuts year on year, and so a lot of the initiatives that have been introduced that we know have been really effective for students, local authorities are really going to struggle to continue with those, post this funding going....*
>
> *We will do what we can. We will keep the core bits that we know have been effective, you know, and I think it's right that we do that. But we have to balance our books, just as the local authority does, so we'll just try and do what we can and that's where it's really difficult.'*

Chapter 10 summary

In this chapter, I have looked at some of the ways in which social work is organised, broadly across the period from 1990 to the present, through the development of professional organisation(s), research conferences and some developments in social work/social care education. Using some specific examples has revealed the influences of the state in England and elsewhere in Europe, as well as the role of international networks and organisations, especially in social work research and education.

Notes

[1] I acknowledge the work of my colleagues Rosslyn Webber, Jim Jenkins and Colin Whittington in jointly undertaking this survey project.

[2] Writing about care policy, Freeman (2017: 196) usefully suggests that 'the practices of care–policy in the office and in the field seem to fit with each other only imperfectly, if at all'.

[3] Entitled 'Social Work Education and the Community Care Revolution'.

[4] I would emphasise again here that being culturally competent when working with people (acknowledging and working with differences and diversity) is promoted as a key strength of social work, as well as in health care (see, for example, Papadopoulos, 2006).

[5] See also a recent report of a project connected to one Teaching Partnership in which I have participated with colleagues (Hingley-Jones et al, 2019).

11

Symbolising: cultural representations in theory and in practice

In this chapter, I want to explore some ideas relating to symbols and what we might term 'cultural representation' in social work; in doing this, I will be reflecting on various narratives and experiences gleaned from my informants and/or that I have experienced myself, including material already discussed in previous chapters. Such reflection brings us back to the purpose I expressed in Chapter 2, which was to construct 'a dialogue between those under the scrutiny of anthropologists on the one hand, and anthropologists themselves on the other' (Barnard, 2000: 177).

There is a long tradition in anthropology of the study of symbolising (semiology) (for a review, see, for example, Turner, 1975). These ideas have developed across anthropology, with anthropologists such as Victor Turner (1969) and Mary Douglas (1986; 1999) becoming well known for their explorations into the analysis of symbols, including those used in ritual and in classification systems; these focused mainly on *cognitive* understandings from all kinds of societies. Douglas (1986), in particular, applied ideas such as her developing grid and group classification(s) to various settings, including organisations in Westernised societies. Interestingly, she has also spoken of the ways in which some anthropologists have used exemplars 'in order to *avoid a distinction* between real and symbolic' (Douglas, 1999: 292, emphasis added). The anthropologist Byron Good, whose work with doctors I have already discussed, says that he eschews reality prior to interpretation, and suggests that, for example, medical knowledge in various contexts is 'knowledge of distinctive aspects of reality *mediated by symbolic forms and interpretive practices*. Each depends upon a form of correspondence between language and the empirical world ... [that is,] that which is found within human experience' (Good, 1994: 176, emphasis added).

Being inevitably concerned with diversity and difference (similarly to social workers, in fact), anthropologists such as Good try to use what they identify as symbolic forms to understand and interpret what is going on in another culture. In order to do so, they are therefore dependent on the idea that there is a cultural explanation to be found, and perhaps this can also be seen as distinct from actual reality.[1] As already discussed in Chapter 2, I am aware of the limitations of the notion of 'culture', especially if we were to use this as a broad category in relation to social work overall (see Kuper, 2000). Some researchers have, for example, critiqued the recent ontological approaches to anthropology for reflecting a continuing colonialism within a Euro-centric academy, which can also involve the unfair appropriation of indigenous people's ideas (see Todd, 2016).

However, the idea of working with *cognitive explanations* (asking what and why social workers say they do what they do) can, I feel, still be useful here. I have also, I suppose, enhanced this line of reasoning by casting myself in the role of an outsider who asks questions of social work throughout this book. Good seems to suggest that while the *meaning* of something can be interpreted in different ways, we may also think that the actual object or thing itself remains the same. For example, Good suggests that medical students 'see' (and interpret) the body differently from those who have not received medical training; yet, we may think that the body will surely be the same regardless of who sees it (that is, following a logic of juxtaposing 'culture' and 'nature'). Such logic itself would surely rely mainly on the idea of cognitive explanations, involving signs (for example, as expressed in specific language) and symbols, yet it could also include social action.[2] According to the anthropologist Turner's (1975: 154) designation, 'signs' should be distinguished from 'symbols', the former being mainly 'univocal' and 'almost always organized in "closed" systems ... [owing] their "meaning" to positional relationships'. Turner (1975: 155) identifies the contrasting properties of 'symbols' as 'multivocality, complexity of association, ambiguity, open-endedness, primacy of feeling and willing over thinking in their semantics, their propensity to ramify into further semantic subsystems ... [that are] connected with their dynamic quality'. Furthermore, he suggests that 'Symbols are triggers of social action ... and of personal action in the public arena' (Turner, 1975: 155).

I would designate 'cultural representation' to cover issues of 'signs', including language, as well as 'symbols'. One of the things that people seem to associate with professionals, including social workers, is their use of language and particularly *jargon* in verbal or written forms; this is often associated with their uses of power and exclusiveness in relation to outsiders (see, for example, Hafford-Letchfield, 2015: 66–7). For example, in Chapter 5, I gave one example of how social workers unsuccessfully tried to explain a job title to users of their services before realising they were using jargon. Another personal example from my experience can illustrate professional uses of jargon. The meaning of this linguistic term (Or 'sign'?) was easily resolved once I had understood the abbreviation.

Box 11.1: An exclusionary acronym?

When attending a day conference in the early 1990s (in order to represent our research project with my colleagues), I began to realise that my lack of appropriate background left me unprepared to understand some of the key issues that people were discussing. Speaker after speaker kept referring to 'SSI, SSI': I was completely in the dark until someone helpfully said, 'Social Services Inspectorate'.

In Chapter 10, we discussed some of the implications that arose from dividing organisations and individuals into 'purchasers' and 'providers' of UK services and training in the context of Community Care policy changes. As I described, trying to implement these labels in practice proved difficult, which suggests not only that these terms were ambiguous, but also that they had symbolic aspects underpinned by an adherence to an explicit business ideology, as much as being any reflection of people's real experiences.

Returning to the idea of interpretations and reality, as I have got used to working with social workers, I have become accustomed to them using various terms, such as 'service users' (sometimes also called 'the people we serve') or even the term 'families', which also seem to be ambiguous labels when examined. Despite the emphasis given to issues of diversity and difference within social work (see, for example, Wilks, 2015), do social workers understand and represent these linguistic terms in ways that I (or others outside social work, including users of services) would also recognise? Are we all talking about the same things when we use these terms? What might these terms be symbolic of? This issue has encouraged me to explore the usefulness of seeing these terms as culturally representative and symbolic concepts.

We have already seen in Chapter 7 that ethics and values are very important in social work; prompting social workers and students to reflect on and explore their own values by means of symbolic forms can thus be useful and relevant. For example, some social workers and educators, while identifying the usefulness of arts-based approaches for teaching students, have suggested discussing objects as useful symbols for exploring and understanding aspects of social work and social care (see, for example, Couchman et al, 2014). Another example that I have recently come across is the use of prepared narratives from fairy tales to explore ethical issues with social work students.[3]

There has been a changing focus in anthropology back onto *material culture* in recent years, also linking it to other disciplines. This has allowed the exploration of specific objects and artefacts and the meanings attached to them, and this moves the discussion of symbolising from a focus on cognitive understandings to more materialist viewpoints. Anthropologists such as Daniel Miller (2009) have led some of these developments by considering how objects can be constitutive of identity, how objects can actually 'make' subjects. Interestingly, these ideas about objects and artefacts have recently been identified as relevant to social work, especially in relation to social workers' identities, research and everyday work practices (see Scholar, 2017, who cites Miller's work; see also Doel, 2017, 2019).

A large-scale international project focusing on exploring 'social work in 40 objects'[4] (Doel, 2017, 2019) continues the theme of objects as *symbols*. Doel asked people across the world who were involved with social work to identify objects that held significance for them, which we might regard as symbols, and he relates these to issues of identity and storytelling/narrative. He clearly aimed to construct a diverse social work narrative, which it is hoped may increase public as well as professional awareness and understanding, including what Scholar (2017) has identified as 'hidden' or taken-for-granted objects and aspects of social work. Doel has classified all these objects into complex categories of meaning, suggesting how they can be displayed in a 'virtual exhibition', of which he is curator (Doel, 2019). Interestingly, he includes both professional social workers and those who are receiving or using social work services as his 'donors' of objects. One interesting example is jewellery created by a group of users of services 'to show what social work means to them'. Doel teases out individual stories (in a similar way to Miller), stressing that objects do not necessarily speak for themselves, but need to be seen in the context of the person's explanation for inclusion. He constructs a typology of six object categories from the 127 project donations:

- 'metaphorical objects', physical objects that share similarities;
- 'metaphysical' objects, that is, cognitive themes, not necessarily 'material', but representing core elements of social work (Douglas's [1999] focus on exemplars would surely be relevant here);

- 'personal objects', from someone's history (an area covered in particular by Miller's work);
- 'socio-political objects', linking social work and wider society;
- 'historical objects', relevant to the development of social work; and
- 'practical objects' used in direct practice.

In a parallel development apparently taking anthropology in a more radical direction, some anthropologists have suggested that there has been the development of a 'quiet revolution', involving a complex ontological turn (for an overview of the ontological turn, see Heywood, 2017; Holbraad and Pedersen, 2017; Cepek, 2019; for a feminist critique, see Todd, 2016). While I acknowledge all these very interesting developments, I have not been able to ask social workers directly about objects and their symbolic meanings, nor to fully explore the ongoing ramifications of the ontological turn in anthropology. It is nevertheless interesting to reflect on the potential for merging objects and meanings when thinking about symbols and social work.

When reflecting on all these developments, I decided to try and uncover for myself some examples of multi-vocal and ambiguous symbols from my interviews with informants and other research material. To give one example of a potentially symbolic form ('family'), I wondered whether such a term, when used by social workers, could be shorthand for deeper and perhaps more ambiguous meanings: could we not examine such apparently everyday terms as *symbolic* cultural forms? As a previously published example, I have presented an exercise for students (Bell, 2017: ch 8, Exercise 8.1) in which the reader is asked to collect photographs or poems that they can relate to the concept of 'family'; they are then asked to analyse these objects and to explore for themselves what engaging with the exercise reveals about their own attitudes towards family.

The following dialogue was taken from a student focus group, part of the tutor groups project that I have already discussed elsewhere in this book (see also Bell and Villadsen, 2010, 2011). Here, some English postgraduate students are discussing relationships within their own student tutor group, and indicating aspects of trying to build relationships with their fellow student social workers. In doing so, they present 'family' as an ambiguous symbol or object (perhaps what Doel would call 'metaphorical'), with both positive and negative connotations:

Student 3:   *'It takes a long time for people to feel comfortable enough to start talking about stuff. And I think, if you jiggled it up* [that is, moved students around between different tutor groups], *then you'd have to go through that process and actually it could be less, you would achieve even less from it if you had change to, to…. Frankly, I don't know.'*

Student 2:   *'It's really nice about the security.* [Laughs.]'

Student 3:   *'Your little family.* [General laughter.]'

Student 4:   ' *"We are family."*'

Student 2:   *'Yeah, very dysfunctional!'* (See Bell and Villadsen, 2010, 2011)

Clearly, these ambiguous designations of 'family' reach deep into the core themes of social work practice (the laughter is also telling).[5] So, are these students using 'family' as a symbol, linked to the example of their tutor group, for developing a shorthand expressing their shared, collective understanding? Douglas (1999: 298), citing Thomas Kuhn, also suggests that 'the learning of exemplars is part of the process of constituting a community'.

We might also ask how 'family' (as a contested term) (see Ribbens and Edwards, 1998; Robinson, 2012) is treated symbolically in other areas of social work policy and practice. We have already seen in relation to the 'Mothers Apart' project, discussed earlier in Chapter 8, how one practitioner described the supportive (and symbolic) value of holding a 'Mothers' Day' church service for women who had lost children to state care, reporting that women had said that *"nobody acknowledges we are mothers"*. This example also suggests that professionals are here offering a symbolic gift to users of services, which may be intended as part of the process of their empowerment (or, alternatively, professionals are attempting to allow women to express their feelings yet acknowledge that they are *not* mothers day to day – the 'exception that proves the rule').

For another policy example, I have considered material about the influential 'Reclaiming Social Work' practice system developed in the UK for social work with families. In this model, 'family' is clearly seen as part of a system, and social work practice with families is necessarily seen by these authors as collaborative: 'Reclaiming Social Work is a method of practice that is fundamentally connected with collaborative and respectful working, inviting the family and all members of the system [which is said to include other professionals] … to join in finding a solution to the presenting difficulty' (Trowler and Goodman, 2011: 16). This way of working is supposed to allow professionals 'to be confident in the positions they take' while also providing 'a context in which families gain enough confidence to rely on their own strengths and resiliences to play a greater role in finding a solution' (Trowler and Goodman, 2011: 16–17).

This picture implies trying to equalise power between professionals and the family, who can then both act instrumentally (And in their own interests?) as far as possible. To an outsider, this discussion raises several questions, such as what is the definition of 'family' here? How independent is the family perceived to be (by professionals) in relation to the wider system? In other words, where does the system referred to in this example actually begin and end?[6] Would the system always include some professionals for any family (such as those related to universal services, for example, education)? Or, is this a wider system invoked for particular families who are in times of difficulty? These questions might not appear to matter, but a further point that these authors make is, 'In general family systems are self-regulating and can manage most difficulties on their own, or with minimal support' (Trowler and Goodman, 2011: 17). Elsewhere in this piece we read that, 'wherever possible', the aim should be 'limiting the role of the state in families' lives and, when that role needs to be executed that it is done speedily, with depth and decisiveness' (Trowler and Goodman, 2011: 16).

Leaving aside further questions that we already raised about the contested nature of the term 'family' (especially cross-culturally), it appears from this policy example that 'family' is being invoked here as a symbol of how social workers (Or those who employ them?) would ideally like to work with users of services: to encourage them to be as self-sufficient as possible. This is a situation where the (iconic) family can be nurtured and cared for by social workers who can also fulfil their own work with courage and integrity in doing so (with the overall support of the family system). However, if the (particular) family is unable or unwilling to change (to more acceptable behaviour), its members can be swiftly controlled (by agents of the state). Any mistakes that occur during these processes, it is said, can be addressed by 'enhancing the [professional] operating systems so that the risk of repeat error is reduced' (Trowler and Goodman, 2011: 16).

At this point, I want to move into another, linked example of a symbolic cultural representation, which is *professionalism*. Can we also see this concept, like 'family', as symbolic? This issue is more difficult to tease out since the whole of this book relates to issues of professionalism and professionals! However, we have already seen how issues of professionalism are contingent on differing national/ international contexts (see Chapter 3; see also, for example, Weiss-Gal and Welbourne, 2008), and where, at times and in certain places, the state has even sought to abolish social work. (However, this absence of social work could also suggest the symbolic significance of what could be missing.) In Chapter 10, we saw how professionalism seems to be closely linked to issues of public recognition, including both the practical and, I would argue, the symbolic aspects of becoming qualified and being appropriately rewarded financially and with profession-specific responsibilities; the examples given in that chapter from Portugal and Romania show how these issues are now being addressed and developed in those national contexts.

In England, several of my informants commented on the fact that social work now has a protected title and so, they argue, it can thus be publicly perceived as a profession, providing social workers with some *symbolic* (in addition to other kinds of) recognition. As a separate issue, however, the position of practitioners in adult social work (in relation to the Care Act 2014) has recently been addressed by Whittington (2016a, 2016b). Whittington's analysis in his two articles, (Whittington, 2016a; Whittington, 2016b) considering the original (from 2014) and the revised (from 2016) versions of the Statutory Guidance to the Care Act, suggests that by the second revised version, significant content about, and endorsement of, principal social workers (PSWs) had been introduced. A PSW in adult care and support is expected to be appointed 'in every local authority, endorsing the role as 'professional practice lead' (Whittington 2016b; 1998). Whittington discusses in detail the various implications of this endorsement, especially for what he terms 'a social work renaissance'. He suggests that for PSWs, while there is *operational* potential, and there are *definitional* implications, there is also a *symbolic* aspect which:

> springs from the allocation of an entire new sub-section of Guidance to a single profession. The addition increases salience, eclipsing references to other professions and adding to social work's recognised status and authority as a profession working with adults in care and support services, although it will take more profound changes to overturn the enduringly lower status of adult work within social work itself. (Whittington 2016b: 1972)

Here and elsewhere, issues of professional recognition and expertise seem to be closely linked: to become a professional practice lead implies someone with recognised expertise in their field. As we saw in Chapters 9 and 10, how this expertise is constructed and how social workers organise and disseminate their professionalism internationally is complex and multilayered.

Having now looked at two underpinning symbols relating to social work ('family' and 'professionalism'), with the included symbolism in relation to adult social work PSWs in the UK, I want to finish this chapter by considering symbolic aspects of an important element of social work education: *work placements/placement support*. These, it seems to me, have potential not only in terms of symbolism, but also (in anthropological terms) in the use of symbols through a *rite of passage*. As mentioned earlier, Turner (1969, 1975) is an anthropologist who has explored rites of passage,[7] including the use of symbols, in different societies through ritual, as does Barth (1975) in his analysis of Baktaman ritual (which was referred to in Chapter 5). I have already discussed how students in different parts of Europe are usually trained partly through being given placements in work settings during their social work education, often for prescribed amounts of time (see Jones, 2015; see also an informant's description of work placements and support for these within universities in Romania in Chapter 5, as well as work placements and English teaching partnerships in Chapter 10; see also Berry-Lound et al, 2016; Hingley-Jones et al, 2019). Work placements form a crucial part of the rite of passage that students undergo to transition into professional social work, with important elements relating to learning and constructing their knowledge, their identities and appropriate ethics and values (Hafford-Letchfield and Dillon, 2015; Jones, 2015; Bell et al, 2017).

Returning to the descriptions of rites of passage by Barth (1975), in that social context, there is particular importance placed, first, on the 'doing' of rites and other actions, as well as the understanding of various symbols (as objects but also as metaphors or cognitive understandings). Similarly, social work students must 'do' their work practice and also need to embed understandings of various symbols relevant to their work (such as 'family' or 'professionalism', using the above examples) (see, again, Doel, 2017, 2019; Scholar, 2017). In both the Baktaman and social work placement examples, individuals who have successfully completed their rite of passage can then, I would argue, whether as individuals or as part of their community, 'work with' these symbols in their subsequent practice.

Unlike social work students, according to Barth (1975), Baktaman people do not have a tradition of what we might call critical reflexivity (he uses the term 'exegisis'), although it is not clear from his analysis (based firmly in what we might call an earlier 'anthropologist as expert' tradition) what the Baktaman themselves believe about this (see, again, Todd, 2016). As we have already seen, for social work students and professional social workers, reflective practice/reflexivity is of crucial importance (see, for example, Holland, 1999; Butler et al, 2007; Cartney, 2015; Jones, 2015). We saw in Chapter 9 of this book an example of a recently qualified social worker ('Case example A') describing how he reflected on and grappled with the meanings and interpretation of evidence in social work practice. Part of students' critical reflection may also include investing personal significance into various symbolic objects or understandings, especially if encouraged to do so (see Doel, 2017, 2019; Scholar, 2017); this could be achieved via group settings or support, for example, where understandings are shared and constructed collectively.[8] In an earlier publication concerning our 'tutor groups' project (Bell and Villadsen, 2010: 62), we suggested that:

> Tutor groups were ... spaces where 'symbolic' events such as the recent 'Baby Peter'[9] case could be discussed. This case in particular seemed to symbolise many issues around professional accountability, anxiety and identity; and tutors were therefore careful in allowing students space to consider its implications and student (and staff) reactions. In doing so the overall aim seemed to be to consolidate and strengthen students' confidence in their own 'professional' role. 'Expert' tutors ... can nevertheless call upon powerful discourses of risk and professional responsibility to legitimise their authority within these groups. There is a focus on values and personal identity construction which is subjective yet is also tied to a notion of 'professional' identification.

In the same study, we also explored the notion of 'liminality' in relation to rites of passage and tutor groups, where tutor groups can be seen as 'liminal spaces': 'these ambiguous spaces [that] are used to develop initiates as professionals through both practical and symbolic means ... we might go beyond Czarniawska & Mazza's (2003) characterization of liminality in these kinds of contexts as simply "metaphorical" since the "rites of passage" we observed were grounded in tangible practices' (Bell and Villadsen, 2010: 62).

In Chapter 5, we heard students and social work tutors speaking about students needing to have space to reflect on problems encountered during work placements, with some saying that the tutor group lies between the university and the practice placement; this arrangement prevented them from being isolated, as well as enabling them to cope with the emotional demands of social work as experienced in the placement in (what was perceived as) the real world. Students also need to engage with the very broad range of expertise involved in social work as both a practice-based and an academic discipline. This is on public display through the organisation of professional and academic journals and conferences, as we saw in Chapter 9. We saw in Chapter 9 how these activities spill over into cognate disciplines, so that social work makes a valuable contribution to the whole range of social sciences, with similar contributions coming from other directions.

Chapter 11 summary

Exploring symbolism and cultural representation is an important aspect of anthropological enquiry. In this chapter, I have reflected on my own ideas about symbolism, cultural representation and social work, including recent developments such as materialism and the use of objects, as well as the ontological turn in anthropology. I have tried to draw together some examples, using issues drawn from previous chapters, relating to a few key symbols that (in keeping with the uncertainties of social work) are characterised by ambivalence, in particular:

- 'family';
- professionalism; and
- work placements, being relevant to ambiguous, liminal spaces between education and the workplace as part of a rite of passage into professional social work.

Notes

[1] However, some anthropologists associated with what has recently been called the 'ontological turn', drawing upon earlier anthropological work in their ideas and methods, have sought to disrupt the distinctions between actual objects or things and their representation/interpretation (see, for example, Holbraad and Pedersen, 2017).

[2] As the feminist Judith Butler (1990) has already shown when discussing gender and sex, if we assume that gender is a social construct, this may seem to imply that sex is, in contrast, a natural category. However, according to Butler, it is how gender is actively performed in action that produces gender identity.

[3] I am grateful to Dr Brian Melaugh of the National University of Ireland, Maynooth, Ireland, for discussing his ongoing work in this area with me.

4   This project was apparently inspired by Neil MacGregor's work, 'A history of the world in 100 objects' (BBC Radio 4 series, https://www.bbc.co.uk/programmes/b00nrtd2/episodes/downloads). Doel (2019) explains that in the first six months of his project, 127 'objects' were donated from 24 countries in five continents.

5   On laughter and interaction, see, for example, Glenn and Holt (2013).

6   On systems theories including critical perspectives, see Healy (2014: 132–50).

7   See also Van Gennep (1960).

8   Turner (1969: 81) speaks of those involved in liminal settings, among themselves, tending 'to develop an intense comradeship and egalitarianism'.

9   This notorious English case involving a child death (in 2007) was significant here as the event and its aftermath were contemporary with our 'tutor groups' project and discussed by students participating in the research (see also Warner, 2014).

12

Changing: the future – social work in wider society

Through this journey, I have tried to examine social work in both its broad manifestations as a practice-based profession and as an academic discipline. In doing so, I have: focused on what social work informants discussed and explored with me; included what social workers, including students, revealed as participants during some of my earlier research projects, including my work with colleagues; and presented some of my own reactions to all of these responses and dialogues.

I have also drawn upon published research and policy literature to provide readers with some wider understanding of how social work and social workers, as well as those working in related occupations (such as social pedagogy), are said to operate in England and other UK countries, as well as in selected countries in Europe. Inevitably, by focusing to a large extent on how social workers have explained their own views of themselves, my resulting view of social work is a selective and partial one. However, as a counterpart to this, I have tried to use my anthropological background to discuss and explore my own involvement with social work since the early 1990s, while continuing to reflect on and ask what (I hope) are relevant questions when exploring social work.

I expect that all this material still raises issues about what social work is, and who it is for: is social work, for example, essentially a political project that challenges orthodox thoughts on behalf of those who are perceived to be economically disadvantaged (in all kinds of societies)? Is it aiming to bring about (absolute) equality, or fairness, for all citizens? Do social workers try to 'help those who help themselves'? Social workers have sometimes seemed to favour a more universalistic approach to their work (in line with the International Federation of Social Workers [IFSW] definition), even while policy intentions (as well as state and other funding) in some countries seem to expect social work to become ever narrower and more targeted on certain sections of society. Even if, as an anthropologist, I try to reject the idea of an overarching and globalised form of social work culture, there are clearly some key threads running through this narrative.

One issue that arises, for example, from material that I have presented in Chapters 4 and 5, where I discussed individuals' motivations for taking up and becoming socialised into social work, is how far should we continue to regard social work as a professional project? There is a lot of evidence to suggest that social workers want to be professionals and to uphold what they regard as their professional standards and values; many policies and political developments (including the introduction of a protected title of 'social worker') support this view. I was therefore interested to hear at a recent international conference in Flanders (Belgium) that one speaker argued for what was termed a wider definition of social work since, in that local setting, particular value was placed upon community-based work, including voluntary work by a wide range of people in the population, all informed by the views and actions of those who are users of social work services. In such circumstances, having a protected title of 'social worker', it was argued, would seem to be too narrow since this would exclude much useful, active 'social work'.

Perhaps in contrast to this line of argument, others have argued in this book and elsewhere that being regarded as professionals ensures that social workers are appropriately rewarded and recognised for the important work that they do in society. This is not, of course, to say that they cannot also work closely with the users of social work services, as well as with all their other partners, in whichever settings they operate (as we saw in Chapter 8). An issue that was coming to the fore in 1990s' England was the importance of taking good account of the views of service users and to actively involve them, as well as other professions and occupations, with social work and social workers. Relevant published research about such involvement, as I noted, includes work by Beresford et al (2007, 2008), Matka et al (2010) and Cocker and Allain (2011). Underpinning all this work lies the importance of values, which we examined in Chapter 7; as we saw, this is a complex area that depends upon many layers of ethical principles, standards and actions that may not always be easy to determine in practice.

Sometimes during my years of involvement with social work, I have come across social workers appearing to isolate themselves from others, especially from other professionals. However, I can also understand their concerns, particularly that the social aspects of people's lives are arguably becoming dominated by scientific or health-related arguments (as we identified in Chapter 9 when discussing interdisciplinarity) (see, for example, Garrett, 2018). Social workers (Naturally enough?) want to champion 'the social'!

A related aspect of social work discussed by my recent informants and those interviewed elsewhere relates to social workers' and social welfare professionals' sense of *identity*. In Chapter 6, I drew upon theoretical work by Jenkins (2014) and Chandler (2017) to suggest that identity can be both collective and individual, and that different forms of identification can be significant. These theoretical ideas proved useful in that chapter for examining not only social workers' approaches to identity, but also my own. Through this reflection, I was able to understand my own feelings and come to terms with my own sense of isolation and exclusion in relation to social work(ers) at certain times, and I realised how this affects my perceived identity (despite also saying that I rejected the idea of 'working with' my emotions professionally). However, I imagine that to be human is also to be inconsistent! This way of thinking and reflecting is something that I have learnt particularly from my social work colleagues.

I make no excuse for exploring a little more, in Chapter 11, the potentially symbolic aspects of social work, particularly combining this with various anthropological perspectives. Indeed, I was delighted to find when researching for the chapter that some social workers had already got there before me (see, especially, Doel, 2017, 2019; Scholar, 2017). Symbols present powerful messages, and in Chapter 11, we addressed a few that seem relevant not only for individuals, but also for policy and the state, as well as for social work as a collective form of identity. I am sure that there are many more symbols out there for social workers and others to usefully examine, work with and reflect upon.

A tendency that I have noticed is for social workers (as much as the state) to want to bring order out of chaos, and thereby a liking for constructing rules and frameworks for themselves and others. These processes hinge very much on specificities of *language*, as we saw in several earlier chapters. My own experiences of working alongside social workers have been generally positive, but my reactions are tempered by feeling that those rules need to have clarity and the reasons for them, where possible, need to be fully explained. Some of my social worker informants have said that they want to break out of narrow definitions and practices, imposed by the state and others, so as to balance out (I imagine) the features of care and control when working with people in their professional role(s). Yet, these positive intentions are not always easy to get across to people, and users of social work services may sometimes find social workers' approaches difficult to understand. I would urge social workers to continue to ask themselves: how and when should you try (Or not try?) to be 'on their side'?

I have attempted to engage with some key policy debates throughout this narrative, and tried to demonstrate, using selected examples, how much has changed for social work in different settings and over the past 30 years. I also continue to believe that social work can be relevant to all kinds of societies, and at many different levels. In Chapter 10, I juxtaposed two English policy examples in which I had some involvement (educating for Community Care policy and practice in the 1990s, and Teaching Partnerships in 2017–18) in order to try and illustrate how much has changed, especially in terms of policy, within one national setting. However, some of the same issues still seemed to crop up in these two narratives (the role of the state in social work, and also relationships to other fields such as health care, being important examples).

It has seemed to me that social workers are very engaged with the idea of social change and they clearly have high ideals and values in relation to social justice and towards dealing with the increases in a myriad of social problems. Social workers that I recently interviewed were, for example, very aware of how welfare systems are linked to wider economic and political systems:

> '[Different] *social protection systems, all of them rely on the principle that it is through work and through production activity that the wealth will be redistributed and it is through work that state can guarantee money to support … social protection systems. And what we are seeing now is that work is not the main economic factor anymore … we can have more profits with less work. So, work is not any more a way of redistributing wealth and the way in which social protection systems are organised do not count with that kind of change…. So, it creates a big problem for social protection systems, which will affect not only, but mainly will affect, people outside the labour market, people in poverty, vulnerable people, but in the end it affects society as a whole, in how do we understand society, how do we understand collective responsibility and even the concept of citizenship and what does it mean?'* (Portuguese social worker/educator interviewed in 2018)

There are continuing debates about professional issues such as genericism and specialisation in social work and social work education in various countries. In the UK as elsewhere, the impact of serious cases (such as the Baby Peter example [see Chapter 11]), in the view of some social workers, has tended to shape where social work is heading in the 21st century. Writing in 2005, as noted earlier in a retrospective review of genericism and specialisation in social work since 1970 (see Chapter 3), Stevenson (2005) dates the 'era of child protection enquiries' in the UK to 1973, with the publication of the 1974 Department of Health and Social Security report of inquiry into the 'Care and Supervision Provided to Maria Colwell'. Continuing focus on what is now termed 'safeguarding' seems to be related to this public (and media-based) view of what social work is, or should be; this issue was commented on by several of my recent informants. With the advent of social media, this scrutiny can surely only increase (see, for example, Megele and Buzzi 2020).

There are continuing discussions over social work education across Europe, especially in post-Soviet countries that have been rebuilding their profession; yet, closer to home, some of my English informants did not feel that such issues in social work education were currently being fully debated at the national level:

> 'I think one of the things to me as well, when you know your question, which was an interesting one, about what does the future hold … I think part of why it's so hard to know the answer is that what's happening in social work education isn't being openly debated. You know, there's no sort of parliamentary Bill going through, I mean, obviously, there is in terms of change of regulator etc [to 'Social Work England'], but there's no big debate taking place about, should we be generic, or should we be specialists, you know, should we have mostly employment-based, or is there a role for the university? Those debates aren't happening, I think what's happening is change that is coming by stealth, with just a tender here coming out, a tender there, you know, and so it's sort of moving the profession in a way without that big debate taking place.' (Social worker/educator interviewed in 2018)

One issue that writing this book has impressed on me is the overall international reach of social work; this seems fully compatible with its contingent nature, its focus on social justice and its acceptance and understanding of diversity and difference. However, a recent small-scale study of doctoral social work students in the US (Hudson, 2017) suggests not only that they had varied understandings of the term 'social justice', but also that the prevailing and dominant discourse of liberalism could itself be driving a particularly narrow focus to this concept. Hudson's (2017: 1970) view is that (at least in an American context) 'it is unfortunately expected that social work's approach to social justice will continue to reinscribe dominant normativities, such as whiteness and capitalism'.

As we have seen, both as an academic discipline and in terms of its practice, taking a global approach is nevertheless surely a lesson for those in other fields, as the following recently qualified social worker seems to suggest:

> '*I think that social workers must ... are going to have a globalised way to work in Europe or in the States or in Africa or in Asia, and I think that's going to be to work together. I think that the way social work can always be higher, is working together.... We need to work, we need to communicate with people, we need to work as a team.*' (Portuguese social worker speaking in 2018)

To sum up this whole fascinating journey is difficult, but I am going to leave the last word to one of my recent transnational informants, an experienced social worker and social work educator now working in England. Here is the final part of her interview, which I feel is also a good way to end the whole book:

Informant:	'*I think there always will be challenges around for social work and part of that is obtaining funding for the work that we do and that will always be present, whatever the government of the day is, you know, there will always be challenges for social work. But I think it's a fantastic profession and it's worth fighting for and I have not had one boring day in the job, and, you know, I feel absolutely committed to the values and the ethics that are key and central to what social work is ... and social justice is, you know, I spoke about that at the beginning of the interview and I'm going to end with that because I just think it's so powerful to be able to think about the importance of working alongside people and listening to their stories and helping them live the lives that they want to lead, really, and that's what the role of social work is about.*'
Interviewer:	'*Yes, that's a really good way to finish. So thank you very much for that.*'

Chapter 12 summary

In this final chapter, I reflect on why I think social work and social workers continue to be relevant to society on local, national and international levels, and suggest how the process of looking back across the past 30 years demonstrates how much has changed and will continue to change, but that this in itself indicates a form of continuity. Although some observers may continue to predict the demise of real social work, the core activities of the occupation, involving a tension between caring or controlling, have, it seems, always existed. Yet, the value of compassion, in whatever setting, is what social workers always seem to want to exemplify and to encourage in themselves and others by working alongside people.

References

Adkins, L. and Skeggs, B. (eds) (2004) *Feminism after Bourdieu*, Oxford: Blackwell Publishing.

Alber, E. and Drotbohm, H. (eds) (2015) *Anthropological perspectives on care: Work, kinship and the lifecourse*, New York, NY: Palgrave Macmillan.

All Party Parliamentary Group on Social Work (2013) *Inquiry into the State of Social Work report*, Birmingham: BASW (on behalf of the APPGSW).

Antoft, R., Høgsbro, K., Nissen, M.A. and Olesen, S.P. (2017) 'On the unnoticed aspects of professional practice', in B. Blom, L. Evertsson and M. Perlinski (eds) *Social and caring professions in European welfare states*, Bristol: Policy Press, pp 193–207.

Avby, G., Nilsen, P. and Dahlgren, M. (2014) 'Ways of understanding evidence-based practice in social work: a qualitative study', *The British Journal of Social Work*, 44(6): 1366–83.

Bain, K. and Evans, T. (2017) 'Europeanisation and English social work: the migration of German social work practitioners and ideas to England', *The British Journal of Social Work*, 47(7): 2119–36.

Bamford, T. (2015) *A contemporary history of social work: Learning from the past*, Bristol: Policy Press.

Banks, S. (2012) *Ethics and values in social work*, Basingstoke: Palgrave Macmillan.

Barclay, P.M. (1982) *Social Workers: their role and tasks-Working Party Report*, London: Ncvo Publications.

Barnard, A. (2000) *History and theory in anthropology*, Cambridge: Cambridge University Press.

Barth, F. (1975) *Ritual and knowledge among the Baktaman of New Guinea*, New Haven, CT: Yale University Press.

BASW (British Association of Social Workers) England (2015) 'BASW England response to the review of the Professional Capabilities Framework', https://www.basw.co.uk/system/files/resources/basw_84953-3_0.pdf

BASW, Department for Education and Department of Health and Social Care (2018) 'Joint statement on the relationship between the Professional Capabilities Framework (PCF) for social work and the knowledge and skills statements for children and families and adults', https://www.basw.co.uk/sites/default/files/basw-pcf-and-kss-joint-statement.pdf

Beatty, A. (2013) 'Current emotion research in anthropology: reporting the field', *Emotion Review*, 5(4): 414–22.

Bell, L. (1994) 'Castles and bridges: metaphors for looking at social work training', paper given at the Conference on Metaphors in Organisational Theory and Behaviour, Management Centre, King's College, University of London, July.

Bell, L. (1995) 'My child, your child: mothering in a Hertfordshire town in the 1980s', Phd thesis, University of London, https://ethos. bl.uk/OrderDetails.do?uin=uk.bl.ethos.480867

Bell, L. (2007a) 'Training managers: constructing their identities in English health and care agencies', *Equal Opportunities International*, 26(4): 287–304.

Bell, L. (2007b) '"Castle" or "bridge"? Social work, inter-professionalism and managerialism in the UK', paper given at Lulea Techniska Universitet, Department of Work Sciences, Sweden, October.

Bell, L. (2008) 'Practising knowledge: academic-practitioners' narratives of career and identity', in E. Berg, J. Barry, S. Piippola and J. Chandler (eds) *Dilemmas of identity, New Public Management and governance*, Luleå, Sweden: Luleå University of Technology, Department of Human Work Sciences.

Bell, L. (2015) 'Ethics, values and social work identity(ies)', in L. Bell and T. Hafford-Letchfield (eds) *Ethics, values and social work practice*, London: Open University Press/McGraw-Hill Education, pp 37–46.

Bell, L. (2017) *Research methods for social workers*, London: Palgrave/Macmillan.

Bell, L. and Allain, L. (2011) 'Exploring professional stereotypes and learning for interprofessional practice: an example from UK qualifying level social work education', *Social Work Education*, 30(3): 266–80.

Bell, L. and Birch, M. (2007) 'Interweaving academic and professional power in higher education', in V. Gillies and H. Lucey (eds) *Power, knowledge and the academy*, London: Palgrave Macmillan.

Bell, L. and Clancy, C. (2013) 'Postgraduate students learning about research: exploring the attitudes of social work and mental health students in an English university setting', *Social Work and Social Sciences Review*, 16(2): 37–50.

Bell, L. and Hafford-Letchfield, P. (eds) (2015) *Ethics, values and social work practice*, Maidenhead, Berks: Open University Press/McGraw-Hill Education.

Bell, L and Herring, R (2017) '"We've all got our different stories": mothers and project workers speaking about group support for parents who have lost children to care', paper presented at the ESWRA conference, Aalborg, Denmark, April.

Bell, L. and Villadsen, A. (2010) 'The contribution of tutor groups to social work education: an evaluative study', final report, October, Department of Mental Health and Social Work, Middlesex University, ISBN 978 1 85924 320 6.

Bell, L. and Villadsen, A. (2011) '"A sense of belonging": examining how social work students acquire professional values, identities and practice competence through group support', paper presented at the First European Social Work Research Conference, St Catherine's College, Oxford University, March.

Bell, L., Jenkins, J. and Webber, R. (1997) *Review of Community Care training within CCETSW's London and South East England Region*, London: CCETSW, LSEER.

Bell, L., Lewis-Brooke, S., Herring, R., Lehane, L., O'Farrell-Pearce, S., Quinn, K. and So, T. (2016a) 'Mothers apart: an action research project based on partnership between a university and a local authority in London, England', paper presented at the Social Work International Conference (SWIC), Bucharest, Romania, November.

Bell, L., Lewis-Brooke, S., Herring, R., Lehane, L., O'Farrell-Pearce, S., Quinn, K. and So, T. (2016b) 'Mothers' voices: hearing and assessing the contributions of "birth mothers" to the development of social work interventions and family support', paper presented at the Sixth European Conference for Social Work Research, Lisbon, Portugal, April.

Bell, L., Nissen, M. and Vindegg, J. (2017) 'The construction of professional identity in social work: experience, analytical reflection and time', in B. Blom, L. Evertsson and M. Perlinski (eds) *Social and caring professions in European welfare states*, Bristol: Policy Press, pp 37–51.

Bell, L., Lewis-Brooke, S., Herring, R., Lehane, L. and O'Farrell-Pearce, S. (2018) 'Reflecting on "Mothers Apart": what have we learnt from this partnership project since 2014?', paper presented at the Eighth European Conference for Social Work Research, Edinburgh, Scotland, April.

Beresford, P., with Page, L. and Stevens, A. (1994) *Changing the culture: Involving service users in social work education*, CCETSW Paper 32.2, London: Central Council for Education and Training in Social Work.

Beresford, P., Adshead, L. and Croft, S. (2007) *Palliative care, social work and service users: Making life possible*, London: Jessica Kingsley.

Exploring Social Work

Beresford, P., Croft, S. and Adshead, L. (2008) '"We don't see her as a social worker": a service user case study of the importance of the social worker's relationship and humanity', *The British Journal of Social Work*, 38(7): 1388–407.

Berry-Lound, D., Tate, S. and Greatbatch, D. (2016) 'Social work teaching partnership programme pilots: evaluation. Final research report', May, Department for Education.

Bisman, C. (2004) 'Social work values: the moral core of the profession', *The British Journal of Social Work*, 34(1): 109–23.

Blom, B. (2004) 'Specialization in social work practice: effects on interventions in the personal social services', *Journal of Social Work*, 4(1): 25–46.

Blom, B., Evertsson, L. and Perlinski, M. (eds) (2017) *Social and caring professions in European welfare states*, Bristol: Policy Press.

Blyth, E., Shardlow, S., Masson, H., Lyons, K., Shaw, I. and White, S. (2010) 'Measuring the quality of peer-reviewed publications in social work: impact factors – liberation or liability?', *Social Work Education*, 29(2): 120–36.

Boddy, J., Boaz, A., Lupton, C. and Pahl, J. (2006) 'What counts as research? The implications for research governance in social care', *International Journal of Social Research Methodology*, 9(4): 317–30.

Bodley, J. (2012) *Anthropology and contemporary human problems* (6th edn), Lanham, MD: AltaMira Press.

Bowpitt, G. (1998) 'Evangelical Christianity, secular humanism, and the genesis of British social work', *The British Journal of Social Work*, 28(5): 675–93.

Branco, F. (2018) 'Social work education: the Portuguese story in a local and global perspective', *Practice*, 30(4): 271–91.

Brindle, D. (2015) 'What will fill the gap left by the College of Social Work?', *The Guardian*, www.theguardian.com/society/2015/jun/23/college-of-social-work-closure-british-association-of-social-workers

Bryan, A., Hingley-Jones, H. and Ruch, G. (2016) 'Relationship-based practice revisited: editorial', *Journal of Social Work Practice*, 30(3) (Special Issue): 229–33.

Burnham, D. (2011) 'Selective memory: a note on social work historiography', *The British Journal of Social Work*, 41(1): 5–21.

Burnham, D. (2012) *The social worker speaks: A history of social workers through the twentieth century*, London: Ashgate.

Burrell, G. and Morgan, G. (1979) *Sociological paradigms and organisational analysis*, Aldershot: Gower.

180

Butler, A., Ford, D. and Tregaskis, C. (2007) 'Who do we think we are? Self and reflexivity in social work practice', *Qualitative Social Work*, 6(3): 281–99.

Butler, J. (1990) *Gender trouble: Feminism and the subversion of identity*, New York, NY: Routledge.

Bywaters, P., Scourfield, J., Jones, C., Sparks, T., Elliott, M., Hooper, J., McCartan, C., Shapira, M., Bunting, L. and Daniel, B. (2018) 'Child welfare inequalities in the four nations of the UK', *Journal of Social Work*, https://doi.org/10.1177/1468017318793479

Caldwell, K., Coleman, K., Copp, G., Bell, L. and Ghazi, F. (2007) 'Preparing for professional practice: how well does professional training equip health and social care practitioners to engage in evidence-based practice?', *Nurse Education Today*, 27(6): 518–28.

Cameron, C. (2004) 'Social pedagogy and care: Danish and German practice in young people's residential care', *Journal of Social Work*, 4(2): 133–51.

Carey, M. and Foster, V. (2011) 'Introducing deviant social work: contextualizing the limits of radical social work whilst understanding (fragmented) resistance within the social work labour process', *The British Journal of Social Work*, 41(3): 576–93.

Cartney, P. (2015) 'Links between reflective practice, ethics and values', in L. Bell and T. Hafford-Letchfield (eds) *Ethics, values and social work practice*, London: Open University Press/McGraw-Hill Education, pp 47–59.

Carvalho, M.I. (2014) 'Social work and intervention with older people in Portugal: a critical point of view', *European Journal of Social Work*, 17(3): 336–52, http://dx.doi.org/10.1080/13691457.2014.905459

CCETSW (Central Council for Education and Training in Social Work) (1991) *Rules and requirements for the Diploma in Social Work: Paper 30* (rev edn), London: CCETSW.

CCETSW (1997) *Working with service users in social work education and training in social work and social care: Report of a CCETSW project, conference, 21 November 1997*, London: CCETSW.

Cepek, M. (2019) 'Review of: Holbraad, M and & Pedersen, Morten A. (2017) The ontological turn: an anthropological exposition. Cambridge: Cambridge University Press', *Journal of the Royal Anthropological Institute*, 25(1): 199–200.

CESIS (Centro de estudos para a intervençâo social) (2017) 'The support system in Portugal for children deprived of parental care: guardians and foster care', https://www.cesis.org/admin/modulo_projects/upload/files/National_assessment_v2.pdf

Chandler, J. (2017) *Identity at work*, London: Routledge.

Chandler, J., Bell, L., Berg, E. and Barry, J.J. (2015) 'Social work in movement: marketisation, differentiation and managerial performativity in Sweden and England', *International Journal of Social Work and Human Services Practice*, 3(3): 109–17.

Chandler, J., Berg, E., Ellison, M. and Barry, J.J. (2017) 'Reconfiguring professional autonomy? The case of social work in the UK', in B. Blom, L. Evertsson and M. Perlinski (eds) *Social and caring professions in European welfare states*, Bristol: Policy Press, pp 69–81.

Clark, C. (2006) 'Moral character in social work', *The British Journal of Social Work*, 36(1): 75–89, https://doi.org/10.1093/bjsw/bch364

Clarke, J. (ed) (1993) *A crisis in care? Challenges to social work*, London: Sage/The Open University.

Cocker, C. and Allain, L. (eds) (2011) *Advanced social work with children and families*, Exeter: Learning Matters.

Cojocaru, S. (2008) 'Child protection in Romania after the fall of communism: challenges for the development of community social services', *International Journal of Environmental Studies*, 65(4): 515–27.

Cooper, A. (2015) 'Reviving therapeutic social work', *New Associations*, 19: 1–2.

Cornish, S. (2017) 'Social work and the two cultures: the art and science of practice', *Journal of Social Work*, 17(5): 544–59.

Couchman, W., Hafford-Letchfield, T. and Leonard, K. (2014) 'The practice educator as museum guide, art therapist or exhibition curator: a cross-disciplinary analysis of arts-based learning', *Journal of Practice Teaching and Learning*, 12(3): 48–61.

Coulshed, V. and Orme, J. (2012) *Social work practice* (5th edn), Basingstoke: Palgrave Macmillan.

Cousins, M. (2005) *European welfare states: Comparative perspectives*, London: Sage.

Cree, V.E. and Davis, A. (2007) *Social work: Voices from the inside*, Abingdon: Routledge.

Croisdale-Appleby, D. (2014) *Re-visioning social work education: An independent review*, https://assets.publishing.service.gov.uk/government/uploads/system/uploads/attachment_data/file/285788/DCA_Accessible.pdf

Czarniawska, B. and Mazza, C. (2003) 'Consulting as a liminal space', *Human Relations*, 56(3): 267–90.

Davies, J. and Spencer, D. (eds) (2010) *Emotions in the field: The psychology and anthropology of fieldwork experience*, Stanford, CA: Stanford University Press.

Dent, M. and Whitehead, S. (2002) (eds) *Managing professional identities: Knowledge, performativity and the 'new' professional*, London: Routledge.

Department for Children, Schools and Families (2009) *Final report of the Social Work Task Force*, London: HMSO.

Department for Education (2017) *Learning summary 3: Implementing systemic models of social work*, Children's Social Care Innovation Programme, https://innovationcsc.co.uk/wp-content/uploads/2017/11/2.26_Social-Work.pdf

Department of Health (1998) 'Modernising social services: promoting independence, improving protection, raising standards', White Paper, Cm 4169, London: Stationery Office.

Department of Health (2000a) *A quality strategy for social care*, London: HMSO.

Department of Health (2000b) 'Adoption – a new approach', White Paper, Cm 5017, London: Stationery Office.

Department of Health (2001) 'Radical reforms to social work training to raise social care standards', press release 2001/0154, Department of Health.

Dickens, J. (2010) *Social work and social policy: An introduction*, London: Routledge.

Dickens, J. (2011) 'Social work in England at a watershed – as always: from the Seebohm Report to the Social Work Task Force', *The British Journal of Social Work*, 41(1): 22–39.

Dillon, J. (2011) 'Black minority ethnic students navigating their way from access courses to social work programmes: key considerations for the selection of students', *The British Journal of Social Work*, 41(8): 1477–96.

Dix, H., Hollinrake, S. and Meade, J. (2019) *Relationship-based social work with adults*, St Albans: Critical Publishing.

Doel, M. (2017) *Social work in 42 objects (and more)*, Lichfield: Kirwin MacLean Publishing, https://socialworkin40objects.com/

Doel, M. (2019) 'Displaying social work through objects', *The British Journal of Social Work*, 49(3): 824–41.

Douglas, A. (2008) *Partnership working*, London: Routledge.

Douglas, M. (1986) *How institutions think*, New York, NY: Syracuse University Press.

Douglas, M. (1999) *Implicit meanings* (2nd edn), London: Routledge.

Dumbril, G. and Green, J. (2008) 'Indigenous knowledge in the social work academy', *Social Work Education*, 27(5): 489–503.

Edgar, I. and Russell, A. (eds) (2005) *The anthropology of welfare*, London: Taylor and Francis.

Edmondson, D. and King, M. (2016) 'The childcatchers: an exploration of the representations and discourses of social work in UK film and television drama from the 1960s to the present day', *Journal of Social Work*, 16(6): 639–56, https://doi.org/10.1177/1468017316637221

Edwards, R., Gillies, V. and Horsley, N. (2015) 'Brain science and early years policy: hopeful ethos or "cruel optimism"?', *Critical Social Policy*, 35(2): 167–87, https://doi.org/10.1177/0261018315574020

Ehrenreich, J (2014) *The altruistic imagination: a history of social work and social policy in the United States*, Ithaca, NY: Cornell University Press.

Ellis, C. and Bochner, A. (2000) 'Autoethnography, personal narrative, reflexivity: researcher as subject', in N.K. Denzin and Y.S. Lincoln (eds) *Handbook of qualitative research* (2nd edn), New York, NY: Sage, pp 733–68.

Ellis, C., Adams, T.E. and Bochner, A.P. (2011) 'Autoethnography: an overview', *Historical Social Research*, 36(4): 273–90, https://doi.org/10.12759/hsr.36.2011.4.273-290

Eriksson, L. (2014) 'The understandings of social pedagogy from Northern European perspectives', *Journal of Social Work*, 14(2): 165–82.

Esping-Andersen, G. (1990) *The three worlds of welfare capitalism*, Cambridge: Polity Press.

Esping-Andersen, G. (1994) *After the golden age: The future of the welfare state in the new global order*, United Nations Research Institute for Social Development, Occasional Paper No. 7, World Summit for Social Development, UNRISD/OP/94/7.

ESWRA 2019 (2019) 'Home page', ESWRA 2019, 10–12 April, Leuven, Belgium, https://kuleuvencongres.be/ecswr2019

Ferguson, I. (2008) *Reclaiming social work: Challenging neo-liberalism and promoting social justice*, London: Sage.

Ferguson, I. and Lavalette, M. (2004) 'Beyond power discourse: alienation and social work', *The British Journal of Social Work*, 34(3): 297–312, https://doi.org/10.1093/bjsw/bch039

Ferreira, S. (2005) 'The past in the present: Portuguese social security reform', *Social Policy and Society*, 4(3): 331–38.

Ferrera, M. (1996) 'The "southern model" of welfare in social Europe', *Journal of European Social Policy*, 6(1): 17–37.

Freeman, R. (2017) 'Care, policy, knowledge: translating between worlds', *Sociological Review*, 65(2) (supp): 193–200.

Frost, L. (2008) 'Why teach social work students psychosocial studies?', *Social Work Education*, 27(3): 243–61.

Gachoud, D., Albert, M., Kuper, A., Stroud, L. and Reeves, S. (2012) 'Meanings and perceptions of patient-centeredness in social work, nursing and medicine: a comparative study', *Journal of Interprofessional Care*, 26(6): 484–90.

Garrett, P.M. (2014) 'Re-enchanting social work? The emerging "spirit" of social work in an age of economic crisis', *The British Journal of Social Work*, 44(4): 503–21.

Garrett, P.M. (2018) 'Wired; early intervention and the "neuromolecular gaze"', *The British Journal of Social Work*, 48(3): 656–74.

Gieryn, T. (1983) 'Boundary-work and the demarcation of science from non-science: strains and interests in professional ideologies of scientists', *American Sociological Review*, 48(6): 781–95.

Gillies, V. and Lucey, H. (eds) (2007) *Power, knowledge and the academy*, London: Palgrave Macmillan.

Gilligan, R. (1997) 'Beyond permanence: the importance of resilience in child placement practice and planning', *Adoption and Fostering*, 21(1): 12–20.

Gitterman, A. and Germain, C. (2008 [1996]) *The life model of social work practice* (3rd edn), New York, NY: Columbia University Press.

Glenn, P. and Holt, E. (eds) (2013) *Studies of laughter in interaction*, London: Bloomsbury.

Good, B.J. (1994) *Medicine, rationality and experience: An anthropological perspective*, Cambridge: Cambridge University Press.

Gordon, J. (2018) 'The voice of the social worker: a narrative literature review', *The British Journal of Social Work*, 48(5): 1333–50.

Gordon, J. and Cooper, B. (2010) 'Talking knowledge – practising knowledge: a critical best practice approach to how social workers understand and use knowledge in practice', *Practice*, 22(4): 245–57.

Gordon, J. and Dunworth, M. (2017) 'The fall and rise of "use of self"? An exploration of the positioning of use of self in social work education', *Social Work Education*, 36(5): 591–603.

Gray, M. and Fook, J. (2004) 'The quest for a universal social work: some issues and implications', *Social Work Education*, 23(5): 625–644.

Gray, M., Coates, J. and Yellow Bird, M. (eds) (2008) *Indigenous social work around the world: Towards culturally relevant education and practice*, London: Ashgate/Routledge.

Gray, M., Joy, E., Plath, D. and Webb, S. (2014) 'Opinions about evidence: a study of social workers' attitudes towards evidence-based practice', *Journal of Social Work*, 14(1): 23–40.

Griffiths, R (1988) *Community Care: Agenda for Action. A report to the Secretary of State for Social Services*. London: HMSO.

Griffiths Report (1989) *Caring for people: Community Care in the next decade and beyond*, Cm 849, London: HMSO.

Groves, T. (ed) (1993) *Countdown to Community Care*, London: BMJ Publishing.

Hafford-Letchfield, T. (2015) 'Power', in L. Bell and T. Hafford-Letchfield (eds) *Ethics, values and social work practice*, London: McGraw-Hill Education/Open University Press, pp 63–75.

Hafford-Letchfield, T. and Dillon, J. (2015) 'The contribution of education and learning for ethical practice: situating ethics and values within the social work curriculum', in L. Bell and T. Hafford-Letchfield (eds) *Ethics, values and social work practice*, London: McGraw-Hill Education/Open University Press, pp 23–36.

Hall, D.T. and Chandler, D.E. (2005) 'Psychological success: when the career is a calling', *Journal of Organisational Behavior*, 26(2): 155–76.

Hanna, S. and Lyons, K. (2017) '"London calling": the experiences of international social work recruits working in London', *The British Journal of Social Work*, 47(3): 719–36.

Harris, J. (2008) 'State social work: constructing the present from moments in the past', *The British Journal of Social Work*, 38(4): 662–79.

Hatton, K. (2001) 'Translating values: making sense of different value bases – reflections from Denmark and the UK', *International Journal of Social Research Methodology*, 4(4): 265–78.

Healey, L.M. (2008) *International social work: Professional action in an interdependent world*, Oxford: Oxford University Press.

Healey, L.M. and Link, R.J. (eds) (2011) *Handbook of international social work: Human rights, development and the global profession*, Oxford: Oxford University Press.

Healy, K. (2014) *Social work theories in context: Creating frameworks for practice* (2nd edn), London: Palgrave Macmillan.

Healy, K. (2016) 'After the biomedical technology revolution: where to now for a bio-psycho-social approach to social work?', *The British Journal of Social Work*, 46(5): 1446–62.

Hean, S., McLeod Clark, J., Adams, K. and Humphries, D. (2006) 'Will opposites attract? Similarities and differences in students' perceptions of the stereotype profiles of other health and social care professional groups', *Journal of Interprofessional Care*, 20(2): 162–81.

Heggen, K. and Terum, L. (2017) 'The impact of education on professional identity', in B. Blom, L. Evertsson and M. Perlinski (eds) *Social and caring professions in European welfare states*, Bristol: Policy Press, pp 21–35.

Heinsch, M. and Cribb, A. (2018) 'Just knowledge: can social work's "guilty knowledge" help build a more inclusive knowledge society?', *The British Journal of Social Work*, bcy118, https://doi.org/10.1093/bjsw/bcy118

Hennessey, R. (2011) *Relationship skills in social work*, London: Sage.

Heywood, P. (2017) 'The ontological turn', in *The Cambridge encyclopedia of anthropology*, www.anthroencyclopedia.com/entry/ontological-turn

Higgins, M. (2017) 'Child protection social work in England: how can it be reformed?', *The British Journal of Social Work*, 47(2): 293–307.

Higgs, A. (2015) 'Social justice', in L. Bell and T. Hafford-Letchfield (eds) *Ethics, values and social work practice*, London: Open University Press/McGraw-Hill Education, pp 112–21.

Hingley-Jones, H., Parkinson, C. and Allain, L. (eds) (2017) *Observation in health and social care; applications for learning, research and practice with children and adults*, London: Jessica Kingsley.

Hingley-Jones, H., Allain, L. and Bell, L. (2019) 'Climbing ivory towers? An evaluation of practitioners and academics co-teaching in an English teaching partnership', paper given at the European Association of Schools of Social Work Conference, Madrid, June.

Hockey, J. (2002) 'Interviews as ethnography? Disembodied social interaction in Britain', in N. Rapport (ed) *British subjects: An anthropology of Britain*, Oxford: Berg, pp 209–22.

Hockey, J. (2014) 'The social life of interview material', in C. Smart, J. Hockey and A. James (eds) *The craft of knowledge: Experiences of living with data*, London: Palgrave Macmillan, pp 93–111.

Holbraad, M. and Pedersen, M.A. (2017) *The ontological turn: An anthropological exposition*, Cambridge: Cambridge University Press.

Holland, R. (1999) 'Reflexivity', *Human Relations*, 52(4): 463–84.

Holmström, C. (2010) 'Selection and admission of students for social work education: key issues and debates in relation to practice and policy in England', Higher Education Academy, SWAP report.

Holmström, C. (2014) 'Suitability for professional practice: assessing and developing moral character in social work education', *Social Work Education*, 33(4): 451–68.

Howe, D. (2008) *The emotionally intelligent social worker*, London: Palgrave Macmillan.

Hudson, K. (2017) 'With equality and opportunity for all? Emerging scholars define social justice for social work', *The British Journal of Social Work*, 47(7): 1959–78.

Hughes, G. and Lewis, G. (eds) (1998) *Unsettling welfare: The reconstruction of social policy*, London: Routledge.

Hugman, R (1991) 'Organisation and professionalism: the social work agenda in the 1990s, *The British Journal of Social Work*, 21(3): 199–216.

Hugman, R. (2005) *New approaches to ethics for the caring professions: Taking account of change*, Basingstoke: Palgrave Macmillan.

Hussein, S. (2011) 'Social work qualifications and regulations in European Economic Area. Final report', Social Care Workforce Research Unit, King's College London, report commissioned by the General Social Care Council and Skills for Care and Development.

Hussein, S. (2014) 'Hierarchical challenges to transnational social workers' mobility: the United Kingdom as a destination within an expanding European Union', *The British Journal of Social Work* 44(Supplement 1): i174–92.

Hyare, M. (2015) 'Relationship-based practice', in L. Bell and T. Hafford-Letchfield (eds) *Ethics, values and social work practice*, Maidenhead, Berks: Open University Press/McGraw-Hill Education, pp 101–11.

International Federation of Social Workers (IFSW) (2014) 'Global definition of social work', https://www.ifsw.org/what-is-social-work/global-definition-of-social-work/

Jenkins, R. (2014) *Social identity* (4th edn), London: Routledge.

JUCSWEC (Joint University Council Social Work Education Committee) (2006) 'A Social work research strategy in higher education, 2006 – 2020', London: Social Care Workforce Research Unit, King's College London.

Jones, C. (1996) 'Anti-intellectualism and the peculiarities of British social work education', in N. Parton (ed) *Social theory, social change and social work*, London: Routledge, pp 190–210.

Jones, S. (2015) *Social work practice placements: Critical and reflective approaches*, London: Sage.

Jordan, B. (2000) *Social work and the Third Way: Tough love as social policy*, London: Sage.

Kallio, J., Meeuwisse, A. and Scaramuzzino, R. (2016) 'Social workers' attitudes to privatization in five countries', *Journal of Social Work*, 16(2): 174–95.

Kasza, G.J. (2002) 'The illusion of welfare regimes', *Journal of Social Policy*, 31(2): 271–87.

Kelmshall, H. (2013) 'Risk assessment and risk management', in M. Davies (ed) *The Blackwell companion to social work* (4th edn), London: Wiley Blackwell, pp 333–42.

Kuhn, T.S. (2012) *The structure of scientific revolutions* (4th edn), Chicago, IL: Chicago University Press.

Kuper, A. (2000) *Culture: The anthropologists' account*, Cambridge, MA: Harvard University Press.

Kuper, A. (2016) *Anthropology and anthropologists: The British School in the twentieth century* (4th edn), London: Routledge.

Labonté-Roset, C. (2004) 'Social work education and training in Europe and the Bologna Process', *Social Work and Society*, 2(1): 98–104.

Langan, M. (1998) 'Radical social work', in R. Adams, L. Dominelli and M. Payne (eds) *Social work: Themes, issues and critical debates*, Basingstoke: Macmillan, pp 207–17.

Lazăr, F. (2015) 'Social work and welfare policy in Romania: history and current challenges', *Visioni LatinoAmericane*, 13: 65–82.

Lazăr, F., Mihai, A., Gaba, D., Ciocănel, A., Rentea, G. and Munch, S. (2019) 'Romanian social workers facing the challenges of neo-liberalism', *European Journal of Social Work*, 22(2): 326–37.

Lewis-Brooke, S. and Bradley, N. (2011) 'Family intervention projects: a holistic approach to working with multiple problems', in C. Cocker and L. Allain (eds) *Advanced social work with children and families*, Exeter: Learning Matters, pp 58–74.

Lewis-Brooke, S., Bell, L., Herring, R., Lehane, L., O'Farrell-Pearce, S., Quinn, K. and So, T. (2017) 'Mothers Apart: an action research project based on partnership between a local authority and a university in London, England', *Revista de Asistentă Socială*, XVI(3): 5–15, http://www.swreview.ro/index.pl/numar-3-2017-ro

Lindow, V. and Morris, J. (1995) *Service User Involvement: Synthesis of Findings and Experience in the Field of Community Care*. York: Joseph Rowntree Foundation.

London Community Care Action Group (1994) 'Hearing the voice: assessments of need in Community Care: a practical workbook based on two consultation meetings on needs-led assessments', unpublished.

Lonne, B., Parton, N., Thomson, J. and Harries, M. (2009) *Reforming child protection*, London: Routledge.

Lyons, K.H. (2018) 'Social work education in Europe: a retrospective view', *Practice*, 31(1): 5–19.

Lyons, K. and Orme, J. (1998) 'Research note: the 1996 Research Assessment Exercise and the response of social work academics', *The British Journal of Social Work*, 28(5): 792.

Maidment, J. and Bay, U. (eds) (2012) *Social work in rural Australia: Enabling practice*, Sydney: Allen and Unwin.

Matka, E., River, D., Littlechild, R. and Powell, T. (2010) 'Involving service users and carers in admissions for courses in social work and clinical psychology: cross-disciplinary comparison of practices at the University of Birmingham', *The British Journal of Social Work*, 40(7): 2137–54.

Miller, T., Birch, M., Mauthner, M. and Jessop, J. (eds) (2012), *Ethics in qualitative research* (2nd rev edn), London: Sage.

McDonald, C., Harris, J. and Wintersteen, R. (2003) 'Contingent on context? Social work and the state in Australia, Britain and the USA', *The British Journal of Social Work*, 33(2): 191–208.

Macdonald, G. and Turner, W. (2005) 'An experiment in helping foster carers manage challenging behavior', *The British Journal of Social Work*, 35(8): 1265–82.

McDonald, L. (2013) 'Guest editorial: social work and research methodologies for evaluating interventions', *Social Work and Social Sciences Review*, 16(2): 3–6.

McGregor, K. (2014) 'Is enough attention given to caseloads, supervisions and management during fitness to practise hearings?', *Community Care*, 14 February, www.communitycare.co.uk/2014/02/17/enough-attention-given-caseloads-supervision-management-fitness-practise-hearings/

McLaughlin, K. (2010) 'The social worker versus the General Social Care Council: an analysis of care standards tribunal hearings and decisions', *The British Journal of Social Work*, 40(1): 311–27.

McLaughlin, K., Ferlie, E. and Osborne P.S. (eds) (2001) *New Public Management: Current trends and future prospects*, London: Routledge.

McLaughlin, K., Leigh, J. and Worsley, A. (2016) 'The state of regulation in England: from the General Social Care Council to the Health and Care Professions Council', *The British Journal of Social Work*, 46(4): 825–38.

McNicoll, A. (2016) 'Time to put myths about the College of Social Work closure to bed', *Community Care*, www.communitycare.co.uk/2016/07/14/time-put-myths-college-social-work-closure-bed/

McPhail, B. (2004) 'Setting the record straight: social work is not a female-dominated profession: commentary', *Social Work*, 49(2): 323–6.

Megele, C. (2015) *Psychosocial and relationship based practice*, St Albans: Critical Publishing.

Megele, C. and Buzzi, P. (eds) (2020) *Social media and social work: Implications and opportunities for practice*, Bristol: Policy Press.

Mendes, P. (2005) 'The history of social work in Australia: a critical literature review', *Australian Social Work*, 58(2): 121–31, https://doi.org/10.1111/j.1447-0748.2005.00197.x

Miller, D. (2009) *The comfort of things*, London: Polity.

Miller, S. (2010) 'A conceptual framework for the professional socialization of social workers', *Journal of Human Behavior in the Social Environment*, 20(7): 924–38.

Miller, T. and Bell, L. (2012) 'Consenting to what? Issues of access, gatekeeping and "informed" consent', in T. Miller, M. Birch, M. Mauthner and J. Jessop, (eds) *Ethics in qualitative research* (2nd rev edn), London: Sage.

Miller, T., Birch, M., Mauthner, M. and Jessop, J. (eds) (2012), *Ethics in qualitative research* (2nd rev edn), London: Sage.

Morago, P. (2006) 'Evidence-based practice: from medicine to social work', *European Journal of Social Work*, 9(4): 461–77.

Moriarty, J. and Murray, J. (2007) 'Who wants to be a social worker? Using routine published data to identify trends in the numbers of people applying for and completing social work programmes in England', *The British Journal of Social Work*, 37(4): 715–33.

Moriarty, J., Manthorpe, J., Stevens, M. and Hussein, S. (2015) 'Educators or researchers? Barriers and facilitators to undertaking research among UK social work academics', *The British Journal of Social Work*, 45(6): 1659–77.

Munro, E. (2011) *The Munro review of child protection: Final report*, Cm 8062, London: Department of Education and The Stationery Office.

Murphy, D., Duggan, M. and Joseph, S. (2013) 'Relationship-based social work and its compatibility with the person-centred approach: principled versus instrumental perspectives', *The British Journal of Social Work*, 43(4): 703–19.

Narey, M. (2014) *Making the education of social workers consistently effective. Report of Sir Martin Narey's independent review of the education of children's social workers*, London: Department for Education.

Nurius, P. and Kemp, S. (2014) 'Transdisciplinarity and translation: preparing social work doctoral students for high impact research', *Research on Social Work Practice*, 24(5): 625–35.

O'Brien, M. (2011) 'Equality and fairness: linking social justice and social work practice', *Journal of Social Work*, 11(2): 143–58.

Orme, J., MacIntyre, G., Green Lister, P., Cavanagh, K., Crisp, B., Hussein, S., Manthorpe, J., Moriarty, J., Sharpe, E. and Stevens, M. (2009) 'What (a) difference a degree makes: the evaluation of the new social work degree in England', *The British Journal of Social Work*, 39(1): 161–78.

Ornellas, A., Spolander, G. and Engelbrecht, L.K. (2018) 'The global social work definition: ontology, implications and challenges', *Journal of Social Work*, 18(2): 222–40, https://doi.org/10.1177/1468017316654606

Pálsson, G. (1993) 'Introduction: beyond boundaries', in G. Pálsson (ed) *Beyond boundaries: Understanding, translation and anthropological discourse*, Oxford: Berg.

Papadaki, E. and Papadaki, V. (2008) 'Ethically difficult situations related to organisational conditions: social workers' experiences in Crete, Greece', *Journal of Social Work*, 8(2): 163–80.

Papadopoulos, I. (ed) (2006) *Transcultural health and social care: Development of culturally competent practitioners*, London: Churchill Livingstone.

Parker, R. (1991) *Looking after children: Assessing outcomes in child care: The report of an independent working party established by the Department of Health*, London: HMSO.

Pawlas-Czyz, S., Evertsson, L. and Perlinski, M. (2017) 'The professional development of social work in Poland after 1989', in B. Blom, L. Evertsson and M. Perlinski (eds) *Social and caring professions in European welfare states*, Bristol: Policy Press, pp 147–60.

Payne, M. (2002) 'The role and achievements of a professional association in the late twentieth century: the British Association of Social Workers 1970–2000', *The British Journal of Social Work*, 32(8): 969–95.

Payne, M. (2006) *What is professional social work?* (2nd rev edn), Bristol: Policy Press/BASW.

Perlinski, M., Blom, B. and Morén, S. (2012) 'Different worlds within Swedish personal social services. Social workers' views on conditions for client work in different organisational models', *Social Work and Society*, 10(2).

Perlinski, M., Blom, B. and Evertsson, L. (2017) 'Social and caring professions in European welfare states: trends and challenges', in B. Blom, L. Evertsson and M. Perlinski (eds) *Social and caring professions in European welfare states*, Bristol: Policy Press, pp 253–65.

Philip, G. and Bell, L. (eds) (2017) 'Thinking critically about rapport and collusion in feminist research: relationships, contexts and ethical practice', *Women's Studies International Forum*, 61(2): 71–4, www.sciencedirect.com/science/article/pii/S0277539516303867

Pierson, J. (2011) *Understanding social work: Context and history*, London: McGraw-Hill/Open University Press.

Plafky, C. (2016) 'From neuroscientific research findings to social work practice: a critical description of the knowledge utilization process', *The British Journal of Social Work*, 46(6): 1502–19.

Popper, P (2018) *Social work practice and social welfare policy in the United States: a history*, New York: Oxford University Press.

Portugal (2015) 'Law 142/2015, second revision of the Law for Protecting Children and Young People at Risk', 8 September (Lei n.º 142/2015, segunda revisão à Lei de Proteção de Crianças e Jovens em Perigo), www.cnpcjr.pt/preview_documentos.asp?r=5611&m=PDF

Poso, T., Skivenes, M. and Hestbaek, A. (2014) 'Child protection systems within the Danish, Finnish and Norwegian welfare states – time for a child centric approach?', *European Journal of Social Work*, 17(4): 475–90.

Ravalier, J. (2018) 'UK social workers: working conditions and wellbeing', independent report, Bath Spa University.

Reisch, M. and Andrews, J. (2002) *The road not taken: A history of radical social work in the United States*, New York, NY: Brunner-Routledge.

Research Assessment Exercise (RAE) (2001) 'What is the RAE 2001?' RAE 2001, https://www.rae.ac.uk/2001/AboutUs/

Ribbens, J. and Edwards, R. (eds) (1998) *Feminist dilemmas in qualitative research: Public knowledge and private lives*, London: Sage.

Robinson, L. (2008) *Psychology for social workers: Black perspectives on human development and behavior*, (2nd edn) London: Routledge.

Ruch, G. (2000) 'Self and social work: towards an integrated model of learning', *Journal of Social Work Practice*, 14(2): 99–112.

Ruch, G., Turney, D. and Ward, A. (2018) *Relationship-based social work: Getting to the heart of practice* (2nd edn), London: Jessica Kingsley.

Sapey, B. (2013) 'Compounding the trauma: the coercive treatment of voice hearers', *European Journal of Social Work*, 16(3): 375–90.

Schofield, G. and Beek, M. (2009) 'Growing up in foster care: providing a secure base through adolescence', *Child and Family Social Work*, 14(3): 255–66.

Scholar, H. (2017) 'The neglected paraphernalia of practice? Objects and artefacts in social work identity, practice and research', *Qualitative Social Work*, 16(5): 631–48.

Scurlock-Evans, L. and Upton, D. (2015) 'The role and nature of evidence: a systematic review of social workers' evidence-based practice orientation, attitudes and implementation', *Journal of Evidence-Informed Social Work*, 12(4): 369–99.

Seebohm, F. (1968) *Report of the Committee on Local Authority and Allied Personal Social Services*, Cmn 3703.

Seim, S. and Slettebø, T. (2011) 'Collective participation in child protection services: partnership or tokenism?', *European Journal of Social Work*, 14(4): 497–512.

Sharland, E. (2010) 'Strategic adviser for social work and social care research main report to the ESRC Training and Development Board', https://www.researchcatalogue.esrc.ac.uk/grants/RES-068-31-0001/read/keyfindings

Sharland, E. (2012) 'All together now? Building disciplinary and inter-disciplinary research capacity in social work and social care', *The British Journal of Social Work*, 42(2): 208–26.

Sharland, E. (2013) 'Where are we now? Strengths and limitations of UK social work and social care research', *Social Work and Social Sciences Review*, 16(2): 7–19.

Shaw, I. (2003) 'Critical commentary: cutting edge issues in social work research', *The British Journal of Social Work*, 33(1): 107–16.

Shaw, I. and Lorenz, W. (2016) 'Private troubles or public issues? Challenges for social work research', *European Journal of Social Work*, 19(3/4): 305–9.

Sheppard, M. (1998) 'Practice validity, reflexivity and knowledge for social work', *The British Journal of Social Work*, 28(5): 763–81.

Shore, C. and Wright, S. (1996) 'British anthropology in policy and practice: a review of current work', *Human Organisation*, 55(4): 475–80.

Shore, C. and Wright, S. (2015) 'Audit culture revisited: rankings, ratings and the reassembling of society', *Current Anthropology*, 56(3): 421–44.

Slettebø, T. (2013) 'Partnership with parents of children in care: a study of collective user participation in child protection services', *The British Journal of Social Work*, 43(3): 579–95.

Soydan, H. and Palinkas, L. (2014) *Evidence-based practice in social work: Development of a new professional culture*, Abingdon: Routledge.

Specht, H. and Courtney, M. (1994) *Unfaithful angels: How social work has abandoned its mission*, New York, NY: The Free Press.

Spolander, G., Engelbrecht, L., Martin, L., Strydom, M., Pervova, I., Marjanen, P., Tani, P., Sicora, A., Adaikalam, F. and Tassé, A. (2014) 'The implications of neoliberalism for social work: reflections from a six-country international research collaboration', *International Social Work*, 57(4): 301–12.

Spratt, T., Nett, J., Bromfield, L., Hietamaki, J., Kindler, H. and Ponnert, L. (2015) 'Child protection in Europe: development of an international cross-comparison model to inform national policies and practices', *The British Journal of Social Work*, 45(5): 1508–25.

Staeuble, I. (2006) 'Psychology in the Eurocentric order of the social sciences: colonial constitution, cultural imperialist expansion, postcolonial critique', in A.C. Brock (ed) *Internationalizing the history of psychology*, New York, NY: New York University Press, pp 183–207.

Stevens, M., Moriarty, J., Manthorpe, J., Hussein, S., Sharpe, E., Orme, J., Mcyntyre, G., Cavanagh, K., Green-Lister, P. and Crisp, B. (2010) 'Helping others or a rewarding career? Investigating student motivations to train as social workers in England', *Journal of Social Work*, 12(1): 16–36.

Stevenson, O. (2005) 'Genericism and specialization: the story since 1970', *The British Journal of Social Work*, 35(5): 569–86.

Strathern, M. (ed) (2000) *Audit cultures: Anthropological studies in accountability, ethics and the academy*, London: Routledge.

Strathern, M. (2007) 'Interdisciplinarity: some models from the human sciences', *Interdisciplinary Science Reviews*, 32(2): 123–34.

SWRB (Social Work Reform Board) (2012) 'Building a safe and confident future: maintaining momentum', progress report, Crown Copyright.

Tabin, J.-P. and Perriard, A. (2016) 'Active social policies revisited by social workers', *European Journal of Social Work*, 19(3/4): 441–54.

Tabin, J.-P., Frauenfelder, A., Togni, C. and Keller, V. (2011) 'Whose poor? Social welfare and local political boundaries', *European Journal of Social Work*, 14(4): 463–77.

Tanner, D., Littlechild, R., Duffy, J. and Hayes, D. (2017) '"Making it real": evaluating the impact of service user and carer involvement in social work education', *The British Journal of Social Work*, 47(2): 467–86.

Teater, B., Lefevre, M. and McLaughlin, H. (2018) 'Research activity among UK social work academics', *Journal of Social Work*, 18(1): 85–106.

Terum, L. and Heggen, K. (2016) 'Identification with the social work profession: the impact of education', *The British Journal of Social Work*, 46(4): 839–54.

Thompson, N. (2015) *Understanding social work: Preparing for practice* (4th edn), London: Palgrave.

Todd, Z. (2016) 'An indigenous feminist's take on the ontological turn: "ontology" is just another word for colonialism', *Journal of Historical Sociology*, 29(1): 4–22.

Torfing, J. (1999) 'Workfare with welfare: recent reforms of the Danish welfare state', *Journal of European Social Policy*, 9(1): 5–28.

Trowler, I. and Goodman, S. (eds) (2011) 'A systems methodology for child and family social work', in I. Trowler and S. Goodman (eds) *Social work reclaimed: Innovative frameworks for child and family social work practice*, London: Jessica Kingsley.

Turner, V. (1969) *The ritual process: Structure and anti-structure*, London: Routledge.

Turner, V. (1975) 'Symbolic studies', *Annual Review of Anthropology*, 4: 145–61.

University of Warwick (2012) 'Sources for the history of social work', Modern Records Centre, Information Leaflet Number 13 (revised 7/12), https://warwick.ac.uk/services/library/mrc/explorefurther/subject_guides/social_work

Van Gennep, A (1960) *The rites of passage*, London: Routledge and Kegan Paul.

Villadsen, A., Allain, L., Bell, L. and Hingley-Jones, H. (2012) 'The use of role-play and drama in interprofessional education: an evaluation of a workshop with social work, midwifery, early years and medical students', *Social Work Education*, 31(1): 75–89.

Wallman, S. (1984) *Eight London households*, London: Routledge.

Wallman, S. (1997) 'Appropriate anthropology and the risky inspiration of "Capability" Brown: representations of what, by whom, and to what end?', in A. James, J. Hockey and A. Dawson (eds) After writing culture: Epistemology and praxis in contemporary anthropology, London: Routledge, pp 244–63.

Ward, H. (1995) *Looking after children: Research into practice: The second report to the Department of Health on assessing outcomes in child care*, London: HMSO.

Warner, J (2014) '"Heads must roll"? Emotional politics, the press and the death of Baby P', *The British Journal of Social Work*, 44(6): 1637–53.

Webb, S. (2006) *Social work in a risk society: Social and political perspectives*, London: Palgrave Macmillan.

Webber, M. and Robinson, K. (2012) 'The meaningful involvement of service users and carers in advanced-level post-qualifying social work education: a qualitative study', *The British Journal of Social Work*, 42(7): 1256–74.

Weinstein, J., Whittington, C. and Leiba, T. (eds) (2003) *Collaboration in social work practice*, London: Jessica Kingsley.

Weiss-Gal, I. and Welbourne, P. (2008) 'The professionalisation of social work: a cross-national exploration', *International Journal of Social Welfare*, 17: 281–29.

Weller, S. and Rogers, C. (eds) (2012) *Critical approaches to care: Understanding caring relations, identities and cultures*, London: Routledge.

Whittington, C. (1998) 'Readiness for organisational and inter-professional practice in social work: a sociological study of key contexts and their relevance for qualifying education and training for social workers', PhD thesis, King's College London.

Whittington, C. (2003) 'Learning for collaborative practice with other professions and agencies: a study to inform development of the degree in social work; summary report', Department of Health.

Whittington, C. (2016a) 'The promised liberation of adult social work under England's 2014 Care Act: genuine prospect or false prospectus?', *The British Journal of Social Work*, 46(7): 1942–61.

Whittington, C. (2016b) 'Another step towards the promised liberation of adult social work under England's 2014 Care Act? The implications of revised statutory guidance and the politics of liberation', *The British Journal of Social Work*, 46(7): 1962–80.

Whittington, C. and Bell, L. (1992) 'Selected data from "Learning for work in organisations and with other organisations and professions"', paper given at the Regional Conference on Community Care in the DipSW, CCETSW, London and South-East England Region.

Whittington, C. and Bell, L. (2001) 'Learning for interprofessional and inter-agency practice in the new social work curriculum: evidence from an earlier research study', *Journal of Interprofessional Care*, 15(2): 153–69.

Whittington, C. and Holland, R. (1985) 'A framework for theory in social work', *Issues in Social Work Education*, 5(1): 25–50.

Whittington, C. and Whittington, M. (2015) 'Partnership working, ethics and social work practice', in L. Bell and T. Hafford-Letchfield (eds) *Ethics, values and social work practice*, London: McGraw-Hill Education, pp 76–89.

Wilks, T. (2015) 'Diversity and difference', in L. Bell and T. Hafford-Letchfield (eds) *Ethics, values and social work practice*, London: Open University Press/McGraw-Hill Education, pp 47–59.

Witkin, S.L. (2014) *Narrating social work through autoethnography*, Columbia: Columbia University Press.

Wódz, K. and Falisek, K. (2017) 'State regulation of the social work profession: an example from Poland', in B. Blom, L. Evertsson and M. Perlinski (eds) *Social and caring professions in European welfare states*, Bristol: Policy Press, pp 99–112.

Worsley, A., McLaughlin, K. and Leigh, J. (2017) 'A subject of concern: the experiences of social workers referred to the Health and Care Professions Council', *The British Journal of Social Work*, 47(8): 2421–37.

Index

www.ingramcontent.com/pod-product-compliance
Lightning Source LLC
Chambersburg PA
CBHW070926030426
42336CB00014BA/2552